The OLYMPIC EXPERIENCE in Your School

PARENT-TEACHER COLLECTION

(Grades 4-6)

10 9 8 7 6 5 4 3 2 1

ISBN   1-58000-118-1

TCM   3750

DIRECTOR OF OPERATIONS . . . . Robin L. Howland
PROJECT MANAGER . . . . Bryan K. Howland
AUTHOR . . . . Sarah Kartchner Clark, M.A.
EDITOR . . . . Eric Migliaccio
COVER ARTIST . . . . Brenda DiAntonis
ILLUSTRATOR . . . . Kevin McCarthy
IMAGING . . . . Richard Easley

Published in association with
and distributed by:

Griffin Publishing Group

18022 Cowan, Suite 202
Irvine, CA 92614
www.griffinpublishing.com

Manufactured in the United States of America

Teacher Created Materials, Inc.

6421 Industry Way, Inc.
Westminster, CA 92683
www.teachercreated.com

Table of Contents

Introduction

Dear Educator,

You and your students are about to embark on an exciting exploration of the Olympic Games! Every two years, the world stage opens to the excitement and competition of the Olympic Games. The Olympic spirit permeates the countries of the world and the hearts of the spectators and the athletes. The goal of this book is to capture this spirit and to assist in creating the Olympic experience in your school or classroom.

At the beginning of this unit of study, your students will receive the title of "Olympic Scouts." As Olympic Scouts, they will be ready to explore the Olympic Games firsthand. Your students will learn the history of the Olympic Games and how they are organized. Students will experience teamwork, goal-setting, and hard work. Students will learn about Olympic athletes and their contributions to the story of the Olympic Games. Students will be inspired with past Olympic stories and memories. Finally, the sights and sounds of the Olympic Games will be brought to life with your very own Olympic experience. Olympic Scouts will be involved in the planning, decorating, competing, and reporting of the Olympic Games, and the awarding of the Olympic medals.

This study of the Olympic Games is organized by venues. Each venue contains lessons and activities that span the curriculum and expose students to required skills. Olympic Scouts will work through each Olympic venue. The Olympic venues in this book are as follows:

——————— ☆ **Venue 1: The Olympic History and Traditions**

——————— ☆ **Venue 2: The Olympic Spirit Throughout the World**

——————— ☆ **Venue 3: The Olympic Athlete and Olympic Sports**

——————— ☆ **Venue 4: The Olympic Experience in Your School**

As Olympic Scouts complete the tasks and lessons of each venue, they receive a sticker to put on their Olympic passports. They will each need a completed passport in order to compete in your school or classroom Olympic Games. The experience in each venue will prepare Olympic Scouts to compete in the Olympic Games.

This study will take approximately one month. Each venue will take one week to finish. The culminating week will be the school or classroom Olympic Games. This week should include preparation, as well as the competition aspects of the Olympic Games. Use this book to organize and provide the framework for your own Olympic Games. Feel free to adjust and modify the activities to fit the needs of your students and your school.

The Olympic Experience: An Overview

Here are some suggestions you can use to organize this unit in your classroom. Feel free to alter these suggestions and ideas to meet the needs of your students and your school.

Setting Up the Unit

Begin the preparation of this unit by reading through the venues and the activities. Familiarize yourself with the goals and expectations of this unit. First, read the Olympic Skills and Objectives on pages 6–7 and determine which objectives will be met with this unit. Next, decide which bulletin board or boards you will be using in this unit and get the materials ready. Create a "word wall" in your classroom to post the Olympic vocabulary words from page 12. This will make these words easily accessible for student writing and brainstorming. Make copies of the pages you will need for each week of this unit. Be sure to start off with the Olympic Passport materials on pages 10 and 11. You are ready to begin!

Olympic Scouts

Each student will be given the title of "Olympic Scout" at the beginning of the unit. The goal of an Olympic Scout is to search out information about the Olympic Games. The scouts will complete tasks and assignments in preparation for the Olympic Games. Each Olympic Scout is given a blank Olympic passport. As students travel through the Olympic venues, they are given stickers (page 11) to place on their Olympic passports. Students will need a completed Olympic passport to compete in the Games. See pages 10–11 for the Olympic Passport and the passport pages.

What Is an Olympic Venue?

This unit is divided into sections entitled "venues." Each venue focuses on a different topic related to the Olympic Games. It will take approximately a week to complete the activities and lessons for each venue. At the conclusion of each venue study, students will each collect a sticker to place on their Olympic passports. This provides an easy way to keep track of assignments and projects your students have completed. The culminating activity and the last venue will be the participation in the classroom or school-wide Olympic Games. Read the following brief descriptions of each Olympic venue.

☆ Venue 1: The Olympic History and Traditions

At this venue, students will be learning the history of the Olympic Games and the traditions associated with them. Where were the first Olympic Games held? What do the rings on the Olympic flag symbolize? Why were only men and boys allowed to compete in the first Olympic Games? What is the Olympic torch? What happens at the Opening and Closing ceremonies? All of these questions and more will be answered as students work through this venue. Students will be making their own torches, medals, and other Olympic art and decorations.

The Olympic Experience: An Overview *(cont.)*

☆ **Venue 2: The Olympic Spirit Throughout the World**

Which countries compete in the Olympic Games? What makes each of these countries unique? As students work through this unit, they each are assigned a country to research. Students will learn the customs and traditions of this country. They will also learn of the role this country has played in the Olympic Games. Has this country been an Olympic host? Students will each make a flag of their countries and put together museum displays of artifacts and information about the countries they have studied. Students will study how their countries integrate with the rest of the world, and delegates will be invited to participate in a cultural summit to discuss international topics.

☆ **Venue 3: The Olympic Athlete and Olympic Sports**

At this venue, students will take a closer view of the Olympic athlete. What are the requirements to compete in the Olympic Games? What makes an Olympic athlete great? What skills does an athlete utilize in his or her quest for an Olympic medal? What inner strength is needed? Students will be given an opportunity to examine their own goals and lives in a quest for something greater. Students will also learn about the types of sports in which athletes compete against other athletes. What is the history of these sports? How is a sport admitted as a competitive sport in the Olympic Games?

☆ **Venue 4: The Olympic Experience in Your School**

With the wealth of information the students have about the Olympic Games, they are ready to participate in Olympic sports of their own. At this venue, students will be assigned to a committee. Each committee will be given a specific assignment to play in the Olympic Games in your school. The committees are the following:

➤ *Decorating and Advertising Committee*

➤ *Documenting and Reporting Committee*

➤ *Ceremony Committee*

➤ *Judging and Recording Committee*

➤ *Celebration and Awards Committee*

More information on these committees can be found on pages 74–75. Each committee will also be competing together as a team in the Olympic Games. Students will work together to create teamwork and to win as many medals as they can.

Parent Volunteers

When you are ready to have students compete against each other in the Olympic events, you will want to have parent volunteers on hand to make this run smoothly. You may choose to have a parent meeting to explain the workings of the Olympic Games so that each parent is informed of the role he or she is to play. Try to keep your Olympic Games as organized as possible so that it will be enjoyable for all. For more information on how to organize your own Olympic Games, turn to Venue #4.

Olympic Skills and Objectives

The opportunities for student growth abound in this unit on the Olympic Games. Each subject of the curriculum will be addressed. Here is a list of objectives and skills addressed in this unit:

Language Arts

The students will do the following:

- read for understanding
- establish purpose for reading
- use context clues to determine meaning
- uses story maps and webs
- discuss ideas with peers
- brainstorm and take notes
- use strategies to draft and revise written work
- use strategies to edit and publish written work
- include a beginning, middle, and end in writing
- write a letter including the date, address, greeting, and closing
- write a narrative about a personal experience
- write a biographical sketch of an Olympic athlete
- write a persuasive composition on the Olympic Games
- write a poem about the spirit of the Olympic Games.

Math

The students will do the following:

- use a variety of strategies to solve word problems
- add and subtract numbers with decimals
- understand the basic measures of length, width, height, and weight
- organize and display simple bar or line graphs
- understand the difference between the U.S. Customary and Metric measurement systems.

Life Skills

The students will do the following:

- identify the qualities and characteristics of great Olympic athletes
- identify strategies to foster the positive and supportive characteristics of Olympic athletes
- contribute to overall effort of a group
- use conflict-resolution technique
- use interpersonal communication skills
- set and manage goals.

Olympic Skills and Objectives *(cont.)*

Social Studies

The students will do the following:

- compare and contrast the modern and ancient Olympic Games
- consider how people use ideas from the past to enrich the present
- complete a map of ancient Greece, identifying key locations in the story of the ancient Olympic Games
- analyze the contributions of ancient Greek society in helping to establish the foundations of the ancient Olympic Games
- create suggestions for promoting the spirit of peace in their homes, schools, and communities
- comprehend that each country has customs that are understood and accepted by its people
- study familiar and unfamiliar customs of other nations
- prepare a museum display to help tourists visiting a foreign country
- understand how politics and nationalism have influenced the Olympic Games
- become aware of the lives of children in other countries
- compare and contrast events happening in the world with those happening at home.

Art

The students will do the following:

- know the various purposes for creating works of art
- create art through a variety of mediums and materials
- know how people's experiences can influence the development of artworks.

Physical Education

The students will do the following:

- use a variety of basic locomotor movements (e.g., running, jumping, galloping, hopping, and skipping)
- engage in basic activities that develop cardio-respiratory endurance
- use a variety of basic object control skills
- understand activities that provide personal challenge.

Science

The students will do the following:

- know that the position and motion of an object can be changed by pushing or pulling
- know that an object's motion can be described by tracing and measuring its position over time
- know that friction will slow the speed of an object
- determine the difference between water (liquid), ice (solid), and vapor (gas).

Olympic Bulletin Board Ideas

There are many bulletin board ideas that you can use to bring the Olympic Games into the classroom. Read the following ideas and select the ones that interest you most:

1. If the Olympic Games are taking place at the same time that you are doing this unit, cut pictures and newspaper articles from the newspaper to place on the bulletin board. You can have students complete a Who, What, Where, When, Why, and How outline on what is happening in the news. Post pictures of Olympic athletes and see if students can match the pictures with the names.

2. Make copies of the Olympic pictograms on page 81–85. You can have students write brief reports on each Olympic sport. These can be placed under the pictograms on the bulletin board.

3. Change the bulletin board into a Word Wall by collecting and writing words from or related to the Olympic Games. Students can use this Word Wall as a reference in their own writing projects and assignments.

4. Have students draw pictures of people competing in their favorite Olympic sports. Students can write imaginary journal entries about their day at the Olympic Games. Post the journal entries next to the illustrations.

5. Make copies of the pictograms on pages 81–85. Cut apart the pictures and glue each to a 6" (15 cm) square of red, green, blue, or yellow construction paper. Cover the bulletin board with white paper. Print the words, "The Olympic Games," in large letters across the top center of the bulletin board. Add the labels "Winter" or "Summer" on either side of the board under the Olympic heading. Attach the pictograms under the correct heading, either "Winter" or "Summer."

6. Make a copy of a world map or attach a world map to the bulletin board. As countries compete in the Olympic Games and medals are awarded to the countries, keep a record of the number each country has received. Attach yarn from each country to an index card. Record the medal count for each country on the index card. Change the medal count daily or as the need arises. Use the map to discuss distance, continents, geography, time zones, and the Olympic Games.

7. Read the information on the Ancient Olympic Games on page 15. Discuss them with your students. How are these Olympic Games similar to or different from the Modern Olympic Games? Have students draw a picture taken from the history of the Olympic Games. Post these pictures in correct order on the bulletin board.

Olympic Scout Information

What Is an Olympic Scout?

An Olympic Scout is the title each student receives as he or she begins this unit of study on the Olympics. Make and distribute copies of the Olympic Scout letter at the bottom of this page for each student. You will also need to make copies of the passport cover on page 10. The passport cover can be copied onto cardstock or the copies of the passport cover can be glued to construction paper.

What Is the Olympic Passport?

The Olympic passport is a way to record information on assignments students have completed. It will also serve as documentation that the Olympic Scouts have completed each of the Olympic venues and are ready to compete in the classroom or school-wide Olympics. As the teacher, you can select the assignments you would like your Olympic Scouts to complete.

How to Use the Passport

As you make assignments for the students to complete, have them record these in their passports under the correct venue. Once the assignment has been completed, the date should be recorded. When all of the assignments for a specific venue have been finished, stamp the little box at the bottom right hand corner for each venue of the passport. This can be any stamp you have, or you can choose a symbol to mark off with colored markers. Students must have a completed passport in order to participate in the Student Olympic Games.

Dear Student,

Congratulations! You have just been named an **Olympic Scout.** What is an Olympic Scout? An Olympic Scout is sent to look for clues and information about the Olympic Games, past and present. Try to learn as much information as you can!

As an Olympic Scout, you will use your passport to document the Olympic venues you have visited. There will be assignments to complete before you can have your passport stamped. With a complete passport, you will be ready to compete against other Olympic Scouts in the Olympic Games.

Good Luck!

Olympic Passport

Teacher Note: Give each student a piece of 11" x 17" (28 cm x 43 cm) construction paper. Fold the paper in half. On the cover, glue the Olympic Passport picture to the front. Staple the passport pages (see page 11) to the inside of the passport cover.

Olympic Passport Pages

Directions: Cut along the dotted lines and staple these inside the passport cover on page 10.

Venue 1: The Olympic History and Traditions

Assignment   Date Completed

Venue 2: The Olympic Spirit Throughout the World

Assignment   Date Completed

Venue 3: The Olympic Athlete and Olympic Sports

Assignment   Date Completed

Venue 4: The Olympic Experience in Your School

Assignment   Date Completed

Olympic Vocabulary

There are many words associated with the Olympic Games. Do you know these words? Try using them in your own writing. Feel free to add new words to the list!

(*Teacher Note:* Create a word wall with these words posted so that students can refer to them in their writing and reading.)

amateur: an athlete who competes without monetary compensation

ancient: very old or from long ago

athlete: a person trained in games requiring physical skill, endurance, and strength

bronze medal: a round, decorative piece of bronze (metal) given to the 3rd-place winner(s) in each event

closing ceremony: the program that ends the Olympic Games

compete: to try to win a prize or reward

competitor: people who are trying to win the same prize or reward

event: a contest in a sports program

flag: pieces of material sewn together and decorated with symbols to represent a country or group of people

flame: a fire that burns in the cauldron at the Olympic Games as a symbol of peace between the competing nations

gold medal: a round, decorative piece of gold given to 1st-place winner(s) in each event

Greece: country where the Ancient and Modern Olympic Games were first held

IOC: International Olympic Committee

modern: relating to the present time or time not long past

Olympic Games: a series of international athletic contests held in a host country

Olympic pin: decorative brooch worn to symbolize Olympic events and experiences

Olympic rings: five colored, interconnected rings that symbolize peace among the continents of the world

Olympic torch: a flaming light carried across the world to the Olympic Games

opening ceremony: the program that begins the Olympic Games

play: to take part in a game or exercise

professional: a paid athlete who makes a living competing in sports

qualify: to show the ability or skills needed to be on a team or to participate in a contest

silver medal: a round, decorative piece of silver given to the 2nd-place winner(s) in each event

sport: a physical activity engaged in for pleasure rather than necessity

stade: the length of the Olympic Stadium during the ancient Olympic Games in Olympia, Greece; it is approximately 180 meters

team: a group of athletes working together toward a common goal

USOC: The United States Olympic Committee organizes the Olympic Games and the Olympic Team in the United States

Olympic Trivia

A quick and easy way to share Olympic information is with Olympic trivia. Each day, write one of the following questions on the board. As students enter the classroom, they will read the question and record their answers. Students can work as teams to determine the answer. Remind them it is not about being right or wrong, but making a guess and learning. Reveal the answer later in the day to give students a chance to think about the question. Answers can be found in the answer key on page 94. You can also write trivia questions of your own, or encourage your students to submit trivia questions.

☆ Ancient Olympic Games

1. When were women allowed to compete in the Olympic Games?
2. Who participated in the ancient Olympic Games?
3. In what year did the ancient Olympic Games begin?
4. What did winners in the ancient Olympic Games receive?
5. What is a chariot?
6. What did the ancient judges wear?
7. What did the five rings stand for in ancient Greece?
8. Who first entered the arena during the ancient Games?

☆ Modern Olympic Games

9. What were the only years that the Olympic Games were not held?
10. Which country's team is the first to walk in the Opening Ceremonies?
11. What animal was the first Olympic mascot?
12. What do the rings on the Olympic flag stand for?
13. What must a city have to host the Olympic Winter Games?
14. In which sport did Carl Lewis compete?
15. In which sport did Jim Abbott compete?
16. Name two cities in the United States that have hosted the Olympic Games.
17. What is used to light the Olympic flame?
18. What is the prize for second place at the Olympic Games?
19. How many years are there between the Olympic Games and the Olympic Winter Games?
20. In which country did the modern Olympic Games begin?
21. Who carries the flag of each team into the stadium?
22. Which Olympic Games has more events, summer or winter?
23. Who leads the athletes in reciting the Olympic Oath?
24. What country held the first Olympic Winter Games?
25. What country has hosted the most Olympic Games?
26. What is one of the words in the Olympic motto?
27. Why are doves sometimes released at the Olympic Games?
28. When is the Olympic flame lit?
29. Why did mostly U.S. athletes attend the St. Louis Olympic Games?
30. Name a country that has hosted both Summer and Winter Games.

OLYMPIC VENUE

1

THE OLYMPIC HISTORY AND TRADITIONS

The Ancient Olympic Games

Directions: Read the information on the Ancient Olympic Games. Then answer the questions on the following page.

The accepted date of the first Olympiad is 776 B.C., but some think that Olympic Games were held prior to this date. The first Olympic Games were held in the Valley of Olympia in Greece, which is where the name is derived. Olympia was located in the small "kingdom" of Elis. The first Olympic champion, Coroebus, was a cook from Olympia. These early Olympics were held in a stadium and a temple built to the God Zeus. On the specified day, "a day of games" was held to honor a god or a dead hero. Gods were very important to the people of Olympia and throughout Greece.

The early Olympic Games were a mixture of athleticism, religion, education, culture, and art. The early Greeks strived to improve physically, spiritually, and intellectually. They believed that the gods would help improve their lives. They built an enormous temple in honor of Zeus, who was considered to be the most powerful of the Greek gods.

The first Olympic Games included a foot race, which was also referred to as the stadium race. This race was called the Dromos. The Dromos was a foot race run the length of the stadium. This distance became known as the stade, which was approximately 180 meters or 600 feet. The stade served as the distance used to determine the basic length of future Olympic Game races, even in modern times. Eventually other events were added. Other events included a long distance foot race, wrestling, and the pentathlon. The pentathlon consisted of five events combined. The ancient games ended after the year 934 A.D. because they were viewed by Christians as a pagan ritual. These early Olympic Games had lasted more than 1,000 years.

An Olympic athlete was very strong, both mentally and physically. A Greek athlete would typically eat over six pounds of meat after a day of training. Only men and boys were allowed to compete in these Olympic Games. In time, events were set up for women. These were known as the Herranic Games, in honor of Zeus' wife, Hera. They were held regularly, two years after Olympic Games.

The spirit of peace pervaded the early Olympic Games, as this was a time when the warring cities would set their hostilities aside in what was known as the Olympic truce. This same spirit of peace and unity is important in the Olympic Games of today.

The Ancient
Olympic Games *(cont.)*

Use the previous page to help you answer these questions.

1. List three things that you learned about the ancient Olympic Games.

   _____

   _____

2. How are the ancient Olympic Games different from those of today? List three differences.

   _____

   _____

3. How are the ancient Olympic Games the same as those of today? List three similarities.

   _____

   _____

4. What qualities and virtues were important to ancient Olympic athletes? What qualities and virtues are important to Olympic athletes today?

   _____

   _____

5. The first Olympic Games featured only one event. What was this race called? What was the distance of this race?

   _____

   _____

6. Describe the first Olympic athletes. Who were they? What was their diet? What were their goals and aspirations?

   _____

   _____

7. What was the role of women in the ancient Olympic Games?

   _____

   _____

8. Who was Zeus? What did the people do during the Olympic Games to honor him?

   _____

   _____

An Olympic Invitation

Read the imaginary invitation below. This invitation gives you an idea of what the ancient Olympic Games might have been like. Would you have wanted to participate and attend?

You are invited to attend...

The Next Olympiad!

Date: 580 B.C.
Time Period: Five Days
Place: Valley of Olympia
(see schedule below for details)

Day One

~ Olympic Preparations ~
~ Sacrifices Made to Zeus, King of the Greek Gods ~
~ Olympic Oath (all athletes must attend!) ~
~ Judges Promise To Be Fair and Just ~
~ Trumpeter Contest ~ Athlete Assignments ~

Day Two

~ Sacrifices to the Gods ~
~ Chariot Races (two-wheeled chariots drawn by four horses) ~
~ Bareback Horse Race ~ Pentathlon ~

Day Three

~ Religious Ceremonies ~
~ Great Banquet ~
~ Boys' Competition in Races, Boxing, & Upright Wrestling ~

Day Four

~ Men's Running Events (1-, 2-, and 24-stade races) ~
~ Men's Boxing, Wrestling, & Pancratium ~
(Warning: sometimes deadly. No breaking fingers, biting, or gouging eyes!)
~ Men's Sprint Race in Armor ~

Day Five

~ Sacrifices to the Gods ~
~ Winners Crowned with Olive Leaves ~
~ Athletes' Names, Fathers' Last Names, and Birthplaces Will Be Announced ~

For Your Information:
Women and girls are not allowed to compete or watch for any reason!

Map of Ancient Greece

This is a map of the mainland of ancient Greece. Can you label the cities on the map? Use the city names from the list to fill in the names of the cities on the map below. Some of the letters have been provided for you. Then look at a map of Greece as it appears today. How does it compare with this map?

Olympic Sites and Cities

Athens	Delphi	Mt. Olympus
Corinth	Marathon	Olympia
		Sparta

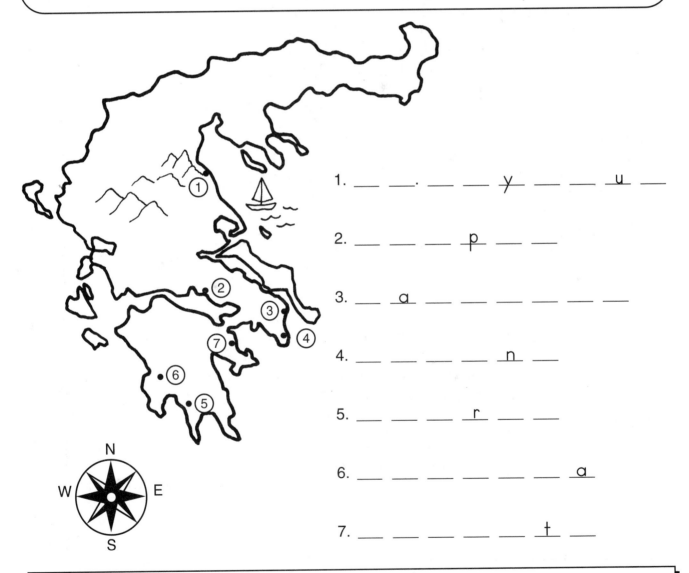

1. __ __ . __ __ __ y __ __ u __

2. __ __ __ __ p __ __ __

3. __ a __ __ __ __ __ __ __

4. __ __ __ __ __ n __

5. __ __ __ __ r __ __

6. __ __ __ __ __ __ __ a __

7. __ __ __ __ __ __ t __

Extension: Research and locate the significance of these cities and sites in ancient Greece. What history do these locations hold? What were each of these places like?

Games in the News

Imagine that you have been assigned to be a reporter of events taking place in the ancient Olympics. Using the information about the ancient Olympic Games on pages 15–18, create a newspaper page reporting the events of the day. Use the newspaper format below for your paper. Be sure that your newspaper page has three news articles, an Olympic cartoon, and a classified section. Give your newspaper a name, too.

The Modern Games

Directions: Read the following information on the Modern Olympic Games.

Credit for the rebirth of the Modern Olympic Games rests solely on the efforts of Baron Pierre de Coubertin. Coubertin became interested in the findings of archaeologists who uncovered and unearthed the city of Olympia, as well as the temple of Zeus. Coubertin believed that an international sports competition could promote world peace. His efforts led to the formation of the International Olympic Games Committee.

The first modern Olympic Games were held in 1896 in Athens, Greece. Since then, with only three exceptions, the Olympic Games have been held every four years. The exceptions occurred during World War I and II.

Through the years, the modern Olympic Games have seen many changes. Transportation was an issue for many of the Olympic Games. Travel was long and hard for many athletes. Transportation in the early years was limited to trains and boats. For this reason, most of the Olympic Games were held in Western Europe because it was easily accessible to fans and Olympic athletes.

In 1900, the sport of polo was introduced, bringing horses back to the Games. The winner's medal was soon cast in gold. Between the years of 1912 and 1948, prizes were awarded in fine arts, as well as in sports. Now, many host cities sponsor a fine arts festival in connection with the Olympic Games. Figure skating and ice hockey were introduced to the Olympic Winter Games in 1924.

The Olympic Games and the Olympic Winter Games were each held in the same year every four years. It wasn't until 1992 that the schedule for the Olympic Games changed. The Olympic Winter Games were held again in 1994 and every four years thereafter. This change allows sports fans and Olympic athletes to compete in and watch the competition every other year.

In 1932, male athletes were housed for the first time in the Olympic Village. Females were housed in nearby hotels. Politics have been present during the Olympic Games, as well. Through the years, countries have boycotted the Games for political reasons. This hurts the athletes who have trained many years to compete.

In 1900, women began to compete in lawn tennis. In 1904, archery was added for women, as was swimming in 1912. Today, women compete for medals in almost all of the events. Technology has also brought changes to the Olympic Games. In 1912, the race results were first aided by electric timers. In 1936, the Olympic Games were first broadcast by radio. By 1960, they received television coverage. Bringing the Olympic Games into the homes of the fans and spectators has helped the popularity of the Olympic Games continue to grow with each competition.

The Modern Games *(cont.)*

Look at the Olympic timeline below. Can you fill in the dates and/or events that are significant to the development of the modern Olympic Games?

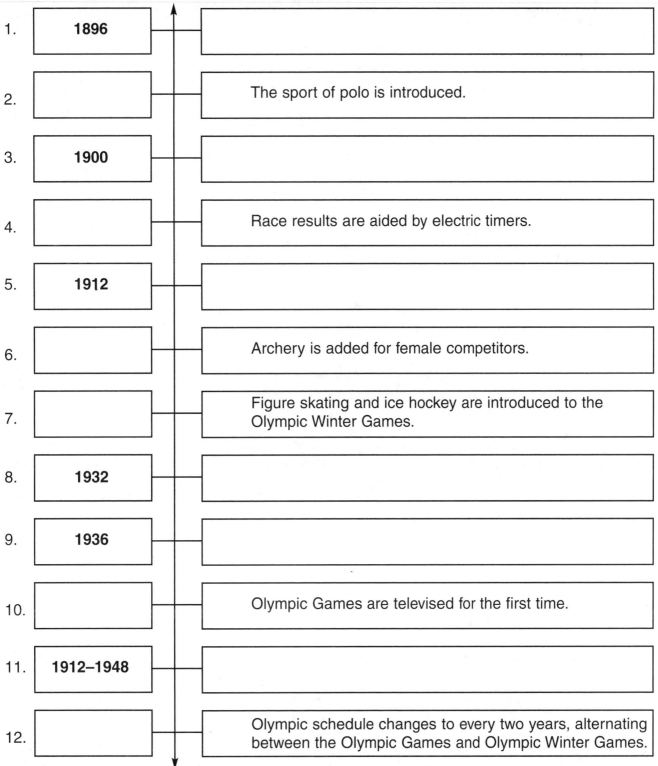

1.	**1896**	
2.		The sport of polo is introduced.
3.	**1900**	
4.		Race results are aided by electric timers.
5.	**1912**	
6.		Archery is added for female competitors.
7.		Figure skating and ice hockey are introduced to the Olympic Winter Games.
8.	**1932**	
9.	**1936**	
10.		Olympic Games are televised for the first time.
11.	**1912–1948**	
12.		Olympic schedule changes to every two years, alternating between the Olympic Games and Olympic Winter Games.

Extension: What recent Olympic events could be added to this timeline? Add two of these to the timeline. Why do you think these events are significant? Share your ideas with the class.

Opening and Closing Ceremonies

❖ Opening Ceremonies

The Opening and Closing Ceremonies of the Olympics have always played a vital role in carrying out the Olympic feel and tone of the Games. The ceremonies are steeped in tradition dating back to the ancient Olympics.

In ancient Greece, the Olympic Games opened with the judges (wearing royal purple robes), a heralder, and a trumpeter entering the Hippodrome. The Hippodrome was the oval track used for the races. The judges took their places and the competitors paraded past them in chariots drawn by four prancing horses. The job of the heralder was to call out the name of each competitor, the name of his father, and his city. When this was finished, the Games were officially open.

The Opening Ceremonies ushered in the modern Olympic Games of 1896, nearly 2,500 years later. This time 258 athletes from 13 different countries paraded into the stadium in Athens, Greece. With more than 70,000 spectators in the stands, the King of Greece declared the Games of the first modern Olympiad officially open.

The Opening and Closing Ceremonies have always been a highlight of the Olympic Games. Each host city stages a spectacular performance of music, dance, and special effects. Local citizens of all ages perform together to welcome the world to their city.

The Parade of Nations begins the opening ceremony. The Greek flag, followed by Greece's athletes, comes first. Next comes the host city's flag and athletes, and then the remaining countries follow in alphabetical order.

Next, there are speeches by the President of the Organizing Committee and the President of the International Olympic Committee (IOC). The Head of State officially declares the Games open. The Olympic flag is raised and the Olympic hymn is played. The Olympic torch is used to light the Olympic flame. Doves are released at this time as a symbol of peace. The Olympic Oath is taken by an athlete and an official. Cultural entertainment is provided by the host city.

❖ Closing Ceremonies

After seventeen days of competition, the Olympic athletes parade into the stadium, but not as countries. Athletes walk in together, competitors walking with competitors. This is done to symbolize the unity and friendship created as a result of the Games. The flags are raised and the national anthems played of three countries: Greece, the current host country, and the next host country. The Olympic flag is passed to the Mayor of the next host city. The President of the IOC pronounces the games closed. The Olympic flame is extinguished, the Olympic flag is lowered, the Olympic hymn played, and more cultural entertainment from the host city is presented.

Olympic Symbols and Traditions

The Olympic Games past and present are filled with symbols and traditions that have stood the test of time. Read about the following symbols and traditions of the Olympic Games.

The Olympic Motto

Citrus, Altius, Fortius

In Latin, these words literally mean, "Faster, Higher, Braver." However, the accepted meaning has become, "Swifter, Higher, Stronger." Father Henri Didon, headmaster of the Aucueil School near Paris, France, wrote these words. The motto represents the athletic ideal of the Olympic Games.

The Olympic Creed

Baron Pierre de Coubertin, the founder of the Modern Olympic Games, created the Olympic creed in 1896. It reads:

"The most important thing in the Olympic Games is not to win but to take part, just as the most important thing in life is not the triumph but the struggle. The essential thing is not to have conquered but to have fought well."

The Olympic Rings

Five interlocking rings represent the five major continents of the world. Their colors—in order from left to right—are blue, yellow, black, green, and red. These colors were used because at least one of them appears in the flag of every nation of the world. These colorful rings are used to symbolize friendship of all humankind.

The plain white background of the Olympic flag is to symbolize peace throughout the games. The colored rings are centered in front of the white background. Though the colors of the rings hold no official significance, some believe that each color represents a particular continent. They feel the black on the flag represents Africa, blue represents Europe, yellow represents Asia, green represents Australia, and red represents North and South America.

The Olympic Athlete's Oath

At each opening ceremony since 1920, a representative of the host country has led the athletes in reciting the Olympic Games oath. The oath is a promise to compete fairly. The words may vary from Olympic Games to Olympic Games, but the spirit remains the same.

"We swear that we will take part in these Olympic Games in the true spirit of sportsmanship and that we will respect and abide by the rules which govern them, in the true spirit of sportsmanship, for the glory of the sport and the honor of our country (or teams)."

Olympic Symbols and Traditions *(cont.)*

The Olympic Torch

The tradition of the modern Olympic torch began in 1936 at the Berlin Games. It was meant to represent a link between the ancient and modern Olympic Games. It has remained an Olympic custom from that time forward.

The torch is lit as it was in ancient times by the sun at Olympia, Greece. The torch is then passed from runner to runner in a relay that travels from city to city across the world until it reaches the host city. It is a privilege and an honor to be selected to carry the Olympic torch. Once the torch reaches the host city, the flame from the torch is used to light a flame in a cauldron at the Olympic Stadium during the Opening Ceremony. The flame burns continuously throughout the Games, and it is extinguished at the Closing Ceremony.

The Olympic Flame

The Olympic flame is lit by the Olympic torch during the Opening Ceremonies of the Olympic Games. The Olympic flame is one of the most visible symbols of the modern games. The tradition of the flame originated in ancient Greece.

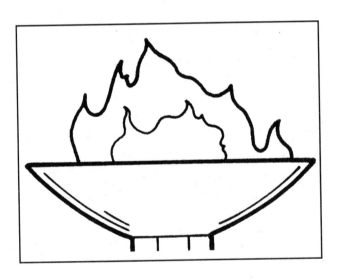

During the ancient Games in Olympia, Greece, a sacred flame ignited by the sun burned continually throughout the games. The tradition of the Olympic flame was first seen in the Modern Games at the 1928 Amsterdam Olympic Games where it burned constantly throughout the games. The flame represents purity, the endeavor for perfection, and the struggle for victory. It also represents peace and friendship.

Olympism in Today's World

What is *Olympism*? This term is new to most Americans. Olympism is the philosophy of the Olympic Movement. It is a set of values that enhances the physical, intellectual, and spiritual growth of participants through sports, art, and music while promoting friendship and understanding in the world.

Olympism offers athletes these things:

- physical and moral development because of the exercise involved and the discipline and control over mind and body required during training and competition

- an attitude of respect for the competitors of other nations

- an appreciation of the beauty of movement that can be transferred into other areas of culture.

The Spirit of Olympism

At each opening ceremony since 1920, a representative from the host country has led the athletes in reciting the Olympic Games Oath. The oath is a promise to compete fairly. The words may vary from Olympic Games to Olympic Games, but the spirit remains the same. The spirit of Olympism encourages the best in the Olympic competitor. It is a set of values that enhances each athlete physically, intellectually, and spiritually. How can the oath and the spirit of Olympism help athletes strive for the best? Answer the following questions.

1. Why is it important to follow the rules of the sport?

_____

_____

_____

2. What does the term "sportsmanship" mean? Explain a time that you have seen it displayed.

_____

_____

_____

3. What are the goals and the purpose of the Olympic Games?

_____

_____

_____

4. How can an athlete improve physically, intellectually, and spiritually by competing in the Olympic Games?

_____

_____

_____

5. What does the phrase, "winning isn't everything" mean?

_____

_____

_____

Medals and Rewards

The awarding of medals and wreaths has been a part of the Olympic Games since the beginning. In the ancient games, an olive branch or wreath represented the highest honor one could receive for winning at the Olympic Games. A heralder would call out the name of the winner, the name of his father, and the name of his city/country. No other prizes were given at the Olympic Games, but when the champion returned home, he often received money and property; sometimes a statue was even built in his honor. Occasionally, an ode to the victor would be written in his honor.

At the first modern Olympic Games in 1896, Olympic champions were awarded gold, silver, or bronze medals. Today, there is a ceremony held for the awarding of medals. The national anthem of the gold medal winner(s) is played and the flag raised. Baron Pierre de Coubertin, father of the modern Olympic Games said, "The most important thing in the Olympic Games is not to win but to take part, just as the most important thing in life is not the triumph but the struggle. The essential thing is not to have conquered but to have fought well." Participating in the Olympic Games is an honor, but winning a medal is every participant's dream.

Imagine that you have been asked to write an ode for an Olympic champion. Write your ode below. Here is an example: *He fought with strength, he fought with might. He showed us endurance, through day and night. And though his medal will not be gold, his story will be gladly told.*

Ode to a Champion

_____

_____

_____

_____

_____

What do you think an Olympic medal should look like? Design a gold, silver, and bronze Olympic medal that would be awarded to an Olympic champion.

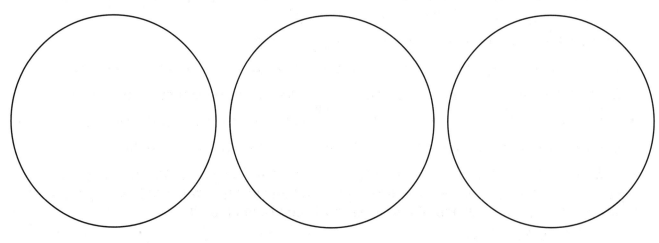

Becoming a Host City

In ancient times, the Olympic Games were held in Olympia, Greece, in the small kingdom of Elis. The first Olympic Games of the modern era were held in Athens, Greece. In 1900, the Olympic Games were held in France—the first time they were held outside of Greece. Since that time, different countries have petitioned to become host cities. This has brought an international feel to the Olympic Games, as each host city/country shares its culture. The International Olympic Committee (IOC) is a group of individuals who decide where the Olympic Games will be held. There are many things to consider. Here are the criteria that the IOC uses to determine the location of the Olympic Games:

- ✧ government support and public opinion
- ✧ city design/transportation
- ✧ sporting sites
- ✧ Olympic Village accommodations
- ✧ environmental conditions and impact
- ✧ security
- ✧ experience from past events
- ✧ finances

1. Using the criteria mentioned, would your city or town be able to host the Olympic Games? Why or why not? _____

_____

_____

2. Write a fictional report to the IOC trying to convince them of the availability of your city to be a host city. Once you have written this report, make a brochure highlighting the strengths of your city.

Name of City: _____

Record strengths in the following areas:

- **Government Support and Public Opinion:** How would the people support the Olympic Games?

- **City Design/Transportation:** Are there roads, freeways, etc. to accommodate traffic? Are there sufficient hotels/motels/places to stay?

- **Sporting Sites:** Are there stadiums, sporting arenas, etc.?

- **Olympic Village Accommodations:** What accommodations will the village have?

- **Environmental Conditions and Impact:** How would the environment be affected?

- **Security:** Can the security of athletes and spectators be guaranteed? What is the plan?

- **Experience from Past Events:** Has this city hosted sports events in the past?

- **Finances:** Does this city have the money to finance an Olympic Games? Is there money available to finance the ceremonies, and any transportation or building changes needed to host the millions of people who will be visiting the city?

Olympic Poetry

Poetry provides you with an opportunity to be creative. Write an Olympic poem using the three formats explained below.

Acrostic Poems

This is an easy poem that doesn't require rhyming! Anacrostic poem is when a word is written vertically. Then you must use each letter in the word for the initial letter of an adjective or phrase that describes the topic. See the box to the right for an example of an acrostic poem. Select a word about the Olympic Games and you are ready to begin!

Only the best athletes

Let the games begin!

Years of hard training

Medals for the winners

Pride in your accomplishments

It's the race of a lifetime

Competing is an honor

Sports for everyone

Cinquain Poems

Use words that describe the ideals of the Olympic Games to write a poem about them. Read the sample cinquain and then try writing one of your own, using the descriptive words you wrote. Try to capture the spirit of the Olympic Games in your cinquain.

Here is the cinquain formula:

Line 1: title *(1 word)*	Olympian
Line 2: description of title *(2 words)*	competitive, strong
Line 3: action about the title *(3 words)*	sweating, trying, pushing
Line 4: feeling about the title *(4 words)*	striving to achieve goals
Line 5: synonym for the title *(1 word)*	greatness

Haiku Poem

Now try writing a haiku that incorporates the feelings of Olympism and the Olympic Games. Read the sample and the formula first. A haiku is three lines in length. The first is five syllables, the second has seven, and the third has five.

five syllables ⟶	Olympic means great
seven syllables ⟶	In spirit, mind, and body.
five syllables ⟶	Ever reaching up.

# OLYMPIC VENUE

2

THE OLYMPIC SPIRIT THROUGHOUT THE WORLD

Olympic Host Cities

Summer

Year	City/Country
1896	Athens, Greece
1900	Paris, France
1904	St. Louis, MO, USA
1908	London, England
1912	Stockholm, Sweden
1916	*not held* (World War I)
1920	Antwerp, Belgium
1924	Paris, France
1928	Amsterdam, The Netherlands
1932	Los Angeles, CA, USA
1936	Berlin, Germany
1940	*not held* (World War II)
1944	*not held* (World War II)
1948	London, England
1952	Helsinki, Finland
1956	Melbourne, Australia
1960	Rome, Italy
1964	Tokyo, Japan
1968	Mexico City, Mexico
1972	Munich, West Germany
1976	Montreal, Canada
1980	Moscow, Russia
1984	Los Angeles, CA, USA
1988	Seoul, South Korea
1992	Barcelona, Spain
1996	Atlanta, GA, USA
2000	Sydney, Australia
2004	Athens, Greece

Winter

Year	City/Country
1896	*not held*
1900	*not held*
1904	*not held*
1908	*not held*
1912	*not held*
1916	*not held*
1920	*not held*
1924	Chamonix, France
1928	St. Moritz, Switzerland
1932	Lake Placid, NY, USA
1936	Garmisch-Patenkirchen, Germany
1940	*not held* (World War II)
1944	*not held* (World War II)
1948	St. Moritz, Switzerland
1952	Oslo, Norway
1956	Cortina, Italy
1960	Squaw Valley, CA, USA
1964	Innsbruck, Austria
1968	Grenoble, France
1972	Sapporo, Japan
1976	Innsbruck, Austria
1980	Lake Placid, NY, USA
1984	Sarajevo, Yugoslavia
1988	Calgary, Canada
1992	Albertville, France
1994	Lillehammer, Norway
1998	Nagano, Japan
2002	Salt Lake City, UT, USA

Extension: What do you think a city needs to have in order to be considered an Olympic host? Make a list of the criteria.

The Countries of
the Olympic Games

On the following pages, you will find some of the flags of host countries where Olympic athletes have competed. Use books and other research materials to identify the flags and write the name of the country above the flag. You will be selecting one of these countries to research further.

1. _____

2. _____

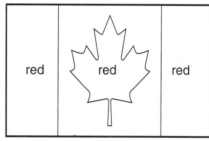

3. _____

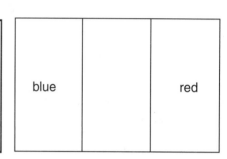

4. _____

5. _____

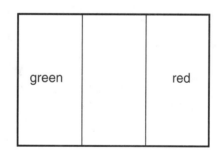

6. _____

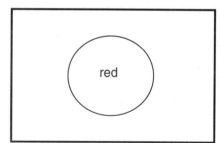

7. _____

31

The Countries of the Olympic Games *(cont.)*

8. _____

red

9. _____

red

navy

10. _____

black	yellow	red

11. _____

blue		blue
	yellow	
blue		blue

12. _____

	dark blue	
dark blue		dark blue
	dark blue	

13. _____

blue | blue
blue
blue | blue
blue
blue

14. _____

green		red

The Countries of the Olympic Games *(cont.)*

15. _____

red

yellow

red

16. _____

red

blue

17. _____

blue

red

18. _____

blue   blue
red   red
blue   blue
red
blue   blue
red   red
blue   blue

19. _____

red   red

blue

red   red

20. _____

red

blue

Country K-W-L

Once you have selected a country of the Olympic Games to research, you are ready to begin. What do you already know about this country? What do you want to know? Are you ready to learn? Fill out the graphic organizer below to organize your previous knowledge and other information. Keep this page handy as you will refer to it later.

K	**W**	**L**
Things I already *know* about this country	Things I *want* to learn about this country	Things I have *learned* about this country

Research an Olympic Country

Select one of the countries that have participated in or have hosted the Olympic Games. You will get to know this country and its culture very well. Be sure to use a variety of resources for your research. Use books, pamphlets, brochures, magazines, newspapers, encyclopedias, almanacs, and the Internet to gather information. You can even request information related to your country through the mail. Use the diagram below to help organize your information. Be sure to let your teacher know the country you will be studying.

My Country: _____

Capital City/Other Cities: _____
_____

Major Religion(s): _____
_____

Foods: _____
_____

Traditions/Holidays: _____
_____

Landscape/Terrain: _____
_____

Famous People from this Country:
_____
_____
_____

Official Currency: _____
_____

Government: _____
_____

Location: _____
_____

Economy/Jobs: _____
_____

Transportation: _____
_____

Olympic Moments/Athletes:
_____
_____
_____

Research an Olympic Country *(cont.)*

Teacher Note: You will be setting up an Olympic Countries Museum. This museum will be a display for students to teach and learn from each other. This museum could be shared with other classes as well and this would give students another opportunity to present their findings and research. Be sure to have enough tables or desks available to hold the museum exhibits.

Option A: Museum Exhibit

Now that you have gathered information on your country, you are ready to share your findings. You will be required to set up a museum exhibit. Be sure to have something representing each of the topics you researched. Here are some ideas you can use:

- map of your country
- flag
- artifacts
- sample music
- recipes
- costumes
- currency
- pictures of the land, people, vegetation
- Olympic moments, memories, athletes

Each country will be placed next to other countries within the same region. Each region will be represented by one of the Olympic rings. For example, all of the countries from North or South America will be grouped together and displayed under the red ring. In the future, you will be meeting with representatives of other countries from this region. Take note as to the similarities and differences of other countries from your region.

Teacher Note: If you feel that you do not have the space for a museum, you can select Option B for students to share their findings and research on their countries.

Option B: Country Presentation

You are also required to make an oral presentation on the country you researched. There are varieties of ways you can present the information you have gathered. You may use one of the following suggestions or one of your own, as long as it is approved by the teacher.

- Draw pictures to hold up as you speak.
- Paint pictures of your country.
- Build a 3-D model of your country.
- Create a large mural of your country.
- Construct a diorama of your country.
- Write a journal of an imaginary sight-seeing trip to your country.
- Put together an informative newscast of your country.

Olympic Cultural Summit

Teacher Note: Once students have researched and presented information on their individual countries, you are ready to assign students to a regional group. The students will represent the countries they have just studied, and countries are divided into groups based on the continent in which they are located. There are five continents represented on the Olympic flag, and so there will be five groups. The continents represented on the flag are Africa, Australia, Europe, North and South America, and Asia. Allow time for students to discuss the questions as a group, and then meet together at a cultural summit to have a class discussion on these topics.

Directions: You will be meeting in groups to discuss the following topics. As you read and discuss the topics, think about what the people from your country might say or how they might feel about it. You will be representing your country, and your group will be representing the region. At the appropriate time, you will be holding an Olympic Cultural Summit as a class to discuss these topics.

- What are the rules required of an athlete competing in the Olympic Games? What is an amateur?

- Should professionals as well as amateurs be allowed to compete?

- Should amateurs be paid for the competition?

- What should be the consequences if an athlete is found using illegal drugs or tests positive for drugs?

- How far do you think an athlete should go to win?

- What do you think of the saying, "Winning is everything"?

- How can you still be considered a winner if you don't come home with a medal?

- Are there any rules about the type of training and help that an athlete can receive?

- What are the pros and cons of holding the Olympic Games?

- What do you think about the safety at the events? Are the athletes and fans well protected?

- What should be the consequences if an athlete is found cheating?

- Do you think it is fair for smaller countries with fewer resources to compete with larger countries with more resources?

- How do you think the Olympic host city should be selected?

- What role do you think politics plays in the Olympic Games? What role should they play?

Now, as a group, write three new questions relating to the Olympic Games that you can bring to the Olympic Cultural Summit. Record these questions below. Be prepared to discuss them at the summit.

1. _____

_____

2. _____

_____

3. _____

_____

Brainstorming Problems and Solutions

Working in the same cultural summit groups created on page 37, assign groups to work through a problem that is associated with the Olympic Games.

1. State the problem or conflict.

   The problem is that the citizens of some countries may not feel that the Olympic Games are fair because they do not have the same funds other countries do to train and prepare their athletes.

2. List those involved in the conflict. _____

   _____

   _____

3. What is the position of each side? _____

   _____

   _____

4. List the possible solutions to the conflict. Brainstorm many possibilities. _____

   _____

   _____

5. Evaluate the solutions. Why do you think some solutions would work, while others may not be as effective? _____

   _____

   _____

6. Decide on the best solution. _____

   _____

   _____

7. Make a list of ways to implement this solution. _____

   _____

   _____

8. Share your findings with the class. _____

   _____

   _____

Extension: As a group, address another problem associated with the countries competing in the Olympics. Use the step-by-step process listed on this page. Share your findings.

Olympic-Sized Problems

There are many issues that need to be addressed when countries begin competing against each other at the Olympic Games. Read through the problems below and then write a possible solution to resolve each conflict.

Conflict A

Several athletes from different countries have been assigned to live next door to each other in the Olympic Village. It is customary for one group of athletes to rise early in the morning to sing praises as part of their religion. Athletes who do not have these customs are awakened very early in the morning to the sounds of the religious ritual. One group of athletes needs to be spiritually in tune to compete at the Olympic Games, while the other group of athletes needs to get the right amount of sleep to compete. What do you think should be done?

_____

_____

_____

Conflict B

On the eve of a sprint race, it has been revealed that an athlete from one country suspects that his competitor from a different country is using illegal drugs. It is against competition rules to take illegal drugs. Word gets out and the press has printed the story in the newspapers. The Olympic officials realize that a false report could ruin the chances for an innocent athlete. What should be done?

_____

_____

_____

Conflict C

Political tension between two competing soccer teams has risen sharply in the days leading up to the Olympics. These two teams are scheduled to play the first game of the Olympic Games. What must Olympic officials do to ensure the safety of athletes, as well as the spectators? What can officials do to ensure that the spirit of peace is still felt at these Olympic Games?

_____

_____

_____

Conflict D

A gymnastics team will be competing as a team, as well as individually in the individual competition. How can the teammates work together towards a common goal as well as compete against each other?

_____

_____

_____

Travel Itinerary

Imagine that you are making a trip to visit an Olympic athlete from the country you have researched. Develop an itinerary for this imaginary trip. What items will you need to take to this country? Is travel permitted freely between your home country and your destination? What documents are necessary to travel to and from this country?

Travel itinerary for: _____
(traveler's name)

Origin of Travel: _____
(city and country)

Destination: _____
(city and country)

Purpose of trip: _____

_____

_____

Travel means: _____

_____
(List all types of transportation necessary: airplane, car, train, bus, boat, etc.)

Hotel Accommodations: _____

_____

Food and Other Expenses: _____

_____

_____

_____

Extension: Invite a guest speaker to come and discuss international travel with your class. What documents are needed to travel to and from foreign countries? What is it like to go through customs? What are the accommodations like in foreign countries?

Graphing the Medals

It is an honor for each of the countries participating in the Olympic Games to win medals. At the end of each day, there is usually a medal count tally to show which country has won the most medals that day. During the first modern Olympic Games, the hosting Greeks were disappointed that they had not yet won a medal in the Olympic stadium. But by the end of the final day, Greek Olympian Spiridon Loues raced into the stadium to win the first Olympic marathon run.

Below is a graph showing the number of medals some countries won during the 2000 Olympic Games. Use the bar graph and answer the questions below.

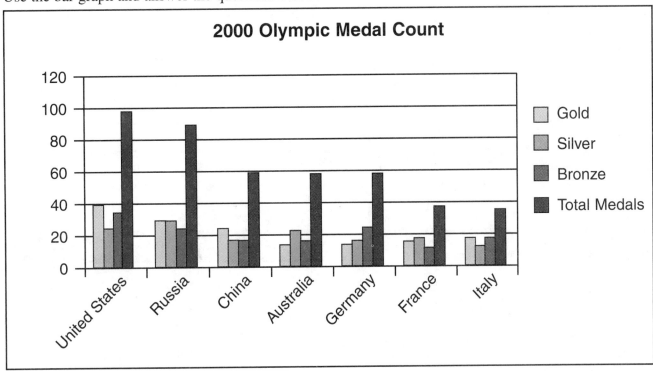

1. Will this graph tell you the names of all the countries participating in the 2000 Olympic Games?

_____

2. What is the purpose of this graph? According to this graph, which country won the most medals?

_____

_____

_____

3. Which country won the most silver medals?_____

4. Which country won fewer bronze medals, Italy or Russia? _____

_____

5. Which three countries won about the same number of total medals?_____

_____

Extension: Make a line graph to show this information. Write five questions that can be answered about your graph.

What Is the Metric System?

In order to measure distance at the Olympic Games, there needs to be a universal measuring system. Since most countries in the world use the Metric System, events are usually measured with the Metric System at the Olympic Games. The U.S. Customary Measuring System uses measurements like pounds, yards, miles, inches, etc. The Metric System uses words such as millimeter, centimeters, meters, grams, and kilograms.

Used in nearly every country in the world, the Metric System was devised by French scientists in the late 18th century to replace the various measuring systems then in use. The Metric System uses the decimal system rather than fractions. To familiarize yourself with the units of the Metric System, go on the Metric Scavenger Hunt.

The Metric Scavenger Hunt

Can you locate objects in your classroom that are these measurements? Remember what these abbreviations mean:

millimeters = mm	**meters = m**	**centimeters = cm**

Metric Length	Name of Object	Actual Measurement
1. 87 cm		
2. 5 m		
3. 240 mm		
4. 66 mm		
5. 1 m		
6. 17 cm		
7. 10 m		
8. 12 mm		

Metric Games

Directions: Divide your class into groups of four or five. Set up a station for each of the Metric Olympic events. Be sure that all of the materials needed at each event/station are available. Students will record each other's measurements. Students will record their results on the space indicated. Assign each group a starting station. Students will rotate through the event/stations. All measurements should be made using metric units.

Materials Needed

- paper plates (4 to 5)
- paper straws (4 to 5)
- cotton balls
- masking tape
- meter sticks (1 for each pair of students, if possible)
- small rulers with metric measurements (1 for each pair of students, if possible)

Standing Long Jump

At this station, make a line with masking tape. Students are to stand on the line and do a standing long jump. Students are allowed two jumps. The longest jump counts.

➢ First Jump   Distance: _____

➢ Second Jump   Distance: _____

Paper Plate Discus

At this event, mark a line with masking tape. Students stand on the line and throw the paper plate like a Frisbee. Students measure the distance the paper plate traveled. Students have two tries to throw the paper plate. The longest throw counts.

➢ First Throw   Distance: _____

➢ Second Throw   Distance: _____

Straw Javelin Throw

This event is set up like the paper plate discus, except the students will be throwing a straw javelin. Students have two throws. The longest throw counts.

➢ First Throw   Distance: _____

➢ Second Throw   Distance: _____

Cotton Ball Shot Put

This event is set up like the paper plate discus, except that students will be using the cotton ball as a shot put. Students have two shot puts. The longest shot counts.

➢ First Throw   Distance: _____

➢ Second Throw   Distance: _____

Time Zones

Another issue that countries throughout the world have to address when competing in the Olympic Games is time zones. In the early days of the modern Olympic Games, many countries were not able to compete because travel was an issue. It was either too expensive or there just weren't the means to travel to certain locations. The luxuries of airline travel were not available and in many places traveling by cars was new and there were few roads on which to travel. Now, Olympic athletes fly all the way around the world to compete in the different countries. Look at the map of time zones and answer the questions below.

TIME ZONE MAP of the WORLD

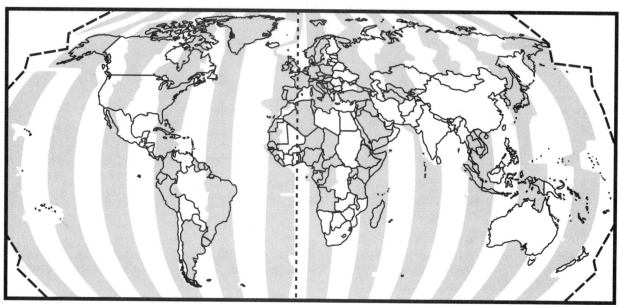

12 am 1 am 2 am 3 am 4 am 5 am 6 am 7 am 8 am 9 am 10 am 11 am NOON 1 pm 2 pm 3 pm 4 pm 5 pm 6 pm 7 pm 8 pm 9 pm 10 pm 11 pm

1. How would jet lag affect the health of an athlete needing to compete?_____

   _____

2. How would time differences impact athletes traveling to training sites prior to the Olympic Games? _____

   _____

3. How would time differences impact an athlete's ability to travel to world class events in preparation for the Olympic Games? _____

   _____

4. How would time differences impact the travel plans of fans and family members coming to watch athletes compete? _____

   _____

44

Money Around the World

There are many expenses involved for countries sending athletes to compete in the Olympic Games. Different countries use different forms of money. The chart below lists the type of money used in each country. Look up the daily exchange rate in the business section of the newspaper or on the Internet or get the information from a local bank. Use the information to fill in the chart and answer the questions below. Imagine that you wanted to spend $500 in American dollars. What equivalent would this be for one of the following countries? Explain how you were able to figure this out.

Country	Type of Money	Exchange Rate
Argentina	Argentine Peso	
Australia	Australian Dollar	
Belgium	Belgian Franc	
Canada	Canadian Dollar	
Chile	Chilean Peso	
Germany	Deutsche Mark	
Great Britain	Pound Sterling	
Italy	Lira	
Japan	Yen	
Norway	Krone	
Russia	Ruble	
Thailand	Baht	

1. Which country did you choose? _____

2. How much money from this country is equivalent to $500 American dollars?

   _____

3. How much money do you think it costs to send one athlete to the Olympic Games? (This will be an estimate!) Explain your answer. _____

   _____

   _____

4. What would affect the price of the Olympic Games for the countries and their athletes?

   _____

   _____

   _____

Olympic Cartoons

In the box below, draw a cartoon that represents an ideal, event, or sentiment related to the Olympic spirit. Can you think of a way to express Olympic friendship, competition, peace, politics, patriotism, or a topic of your choice? Remember it must be related to the Olympic theme. Look at the example. Select your topic and draw your own cartoon below the example. Color your cartoon with colored pencils or crayons. These can be displayed on an Olympic bulletin board.

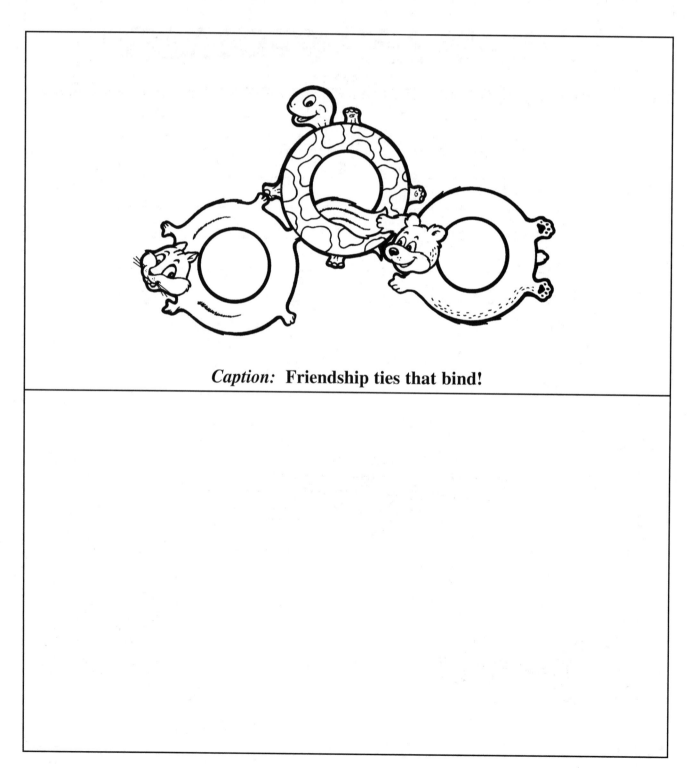

Caption: **Friendship ties that bind!**

OLYMPIC VENUE

1

THE OLYMPIC ATHLETE AND OLYMPIC SPORTS

What Is an Olympic Athlete?

The Olympic spirit begins with the individual athlete. Each athlete comes to the Olympic Games with a unique background. Athletes come from different countries, families, cultures, and training. Yet these athletes have many things in common. They are all reaching for a goal. On the diagram below, list some of the steps an athlete needs to achieve to reach his or her goal at the Olympic Games.

Famous Olympic Athletes

Below is a list of former Olympic athletes. Select one of these athletes to study and write on the line the sport or event in which this athlete competed. Research information about this athlete and how he or she accomplished the Olympic dream. Check with your teacher to see that no one else has selected this athlete to study.

- ❏ Abbott, Jim _____
- ❏ Albright, Tenley _____
- ❏ Balczo, Andras _____
- ❏ Bedard, Myriam _____
- ❏ Blair, Bonnie _____
- ❏ Boston, Ralph _____
- ❏ Calhoun, Lee _____
- ❏ Carpenter-Phinney, Connie _____
- ❏ Clay, Cassius _____
- ❏ Conner, Bart _____
- ❏ Curry, John _____
- ❏ Davenport, William _____
- ❏ Davis, John _____
- ❏ Didrikson, Babe _____
- ❏ Eagan, Eddie _____
- ❏ Evans, Lee _____
- ❏ Fleming, Peggy _____
- ❏ Fraser, Dawn _____
- ❏ Greene, Nancy _____
- ❏ Hamill, Dorothy _____
- ❏ Heiss, Carol _____
- ❏ Jansen, Dan _____
- ❏ Jenner, Bruce _____
- ❏ Jordan, Michael _____
- ❏ Kerrigan, Nancy _____
- ❏ Kjus, Lasse _____
- ❏ Lee, Sammy _____
- ❏ Louganis, Greg _____
- ❏ Mathias, Bob _____
- ❏ McGrath, Matthew J. _____
- ❏ Miller, Shannon _____
- ❏ O'Brien, Dan _____
- ❏ Oerter, Al _____
- ❏ Patterson, Floyd _____
- ❏ Schumann, Carl _____
- ❏ Thorpe, Jim _____
- ❏ Toomey, Bill _____
- ❏ Witt, Katerina _____

- ❏ Akhwiri, John Stehen _____
- ❏ Babashoff, Shirley _____
- ❏ Ballangrud, Ivar _____
- ❏ Biondi, Matt _____
- ❏ Boitano, Brian _____
- ❏ Boucher, Gaetan _____
- ❏ Campbell, Milt _____
- ❏ Caulkins, Tracy _____
- ❏ Comaneci, Nadia _____
- ❏ Connolly, James _____
- ❏ Daehlie, Bjorn _____
- ❏ Davis, Glenn _____
- ❏ deVarona, Donna _____
- ❏ Dillard, Harrison _____
- ❏ Evans, Janet _____
- ❏ Ewry, Ray _____
- ❏ Foreman, George _____
- ❏ Frazier, Joe _____
- ❏ Griffith-Joyner, Florence _____
- ❏ Heiden, Eric _____
- ❏ Henie, Sonja _____
- ❏ Jenkins, David _____
- ❏ Johnson, Rafer _____
- ❏ Joyner-Kersee; Jackie _____
- ❏ Killy, Jean Claude _____
- ❏ Korbut, Olga _____
- ❏ Lewis, Carl _____
- ❏ Masson, Paul _____
- ❏ McCormick, Patricia _____
- ❏ Metcalfe, Ralph _____
- ❏ Nurmi, Paavo _____
- ❏ O'Callaghan, Patrick _____
- ❏ Owens, Jesse _____
- ❏ Retton, Mary Lou _____
- ❏ Thompsen, Daley _____
- ❏ Tomba, Alberto _____
- ❏ Weissmuller, Johnny _____
- ❏ Yamaguchi, Kristy _____

A Tale of an Athlete

Embedded in the history of the Olympic Games are stories that portray commitment, courage, dedication, honor, strength, fitness, and more. Read these inspirational Olympic stories.

❖ Clifton E. Cushman

Clifton Cushman, a renowned track star at the University of Kansas, had won the intermediate hurdles three times at the Kansas Relay and had won the silver medal in the 400-meter hurdles at the 1960 Rome Olympic Games. As Cushman was trying out for the 1964 Olympic team, he stumbled on the last hurdle and fell. This disqualified him from competing on the Olympic team and for a chance to win the gold medal at the Olympic Games. Many students throughout the country wrote to him, telling him how sorry they felt about his unfortunate tumble. He responded with a letter to the youth. Here are excerpts from that letter:

*"Don't feel sorry for me. I feel sorry for some of you! You may have seen me on TV hit the fifth hurdle, fall and lie on the track in an inglorious heap of skinned elbows, bruised hips, torn knees, and injured pride, unsuccessful in my attempt to make the Olympic team…In a split second all the many years of training were…wiped out. But I tried! I would much rather fail knowing I had put forth an honest effort than never to have tried at all."

"…some of you have never known the satisfaction of doing your best in sports, the joy of excelling in class, the wonderful feeling of completing a job, any job, and looking back on it knowing that you have done your best…"

"…I dare you to look up at the stars, not down on the mud, and set your sights on one of them that, up to now, you thought was unattainable. There is plenty of room at the top, but no room for anyone to sit down…"

*Ledeboer, Suzanne. Olympism: A Basic Guide to the History, Ideals, and Sports of the Olympic Movement. *Griffin Publishing Group, 2001.*

❖ The Marathon and Naoko Takahashi

Perhaps the most famous Greek race is the marathon. The marathon distance is 42,195 meters or 26 miles. The marathon was never raced at the Greek Olympic Games. The name actually comes from a legend of a Greek soldier who ran about 22 miles, from the Greek plains of Marathon to Athens, to announce the news of the great victory over the invading Persians. After the soldier made his announcement, the legend says he dropped dead. Though this story may be a myth, its spirit of determination and sacrifice has proven to be inspirational to one of the most famous running events of all time.

The fastest marathon ever run by a woman at the Olympic Games was done by Naoko Takahashi. She ran alone for the last four miles. As she broke the finish-line tape, she raised her arms in triumph. Then she bowed to the crowd. Takahashi overcame 91 percent humidity and won gold in an Olympic-best 2 hours, 23 minutes, 14 seconds to become the first Japanese woman to win an Olympic track and field gold medal. She won a gold medal and she broke the world record! She says she's ready for new goals.

A Tale of an Athlete *(cont.)*

✢ Luz Long and Jesse Owens

Jesse Owens, the son of an Alabama sharecropper, provides another inspirational story. Many people believe that the tone of the 1936 Olympic Games was dampened because the spirit of competition was dominated by Adolf Hitler's politics. Luz Long, a German long jumper, was the athlete that Hitler was counting on. Hitler figured that he could prove his theory that the Aryan race was superior to all others. However, Jesse Owens, an African-American athlete had already won the gold medal in the 100-meter dash. Owens was set to compete against Luz Long in the long jump.

Owens, however, had a difficult time qualifying for the long jump. Owens did what he thought was a practice run, but the officials informed him that it was his first jump. Because of the confusion, Owens was shaken. When he did his second jump, he fouled. Owens had only one jump to go. Long tapped Owens on the shoulder and told him that if he moved his mark back a foot and hit the take-off board, he might qualify.

Owens did qualify, and he also went on to win the finals. He set an Olympic record that day of over 26 feet.

✢ Jim Thorpe

In the 1912 Olympic Games, Jim Thorpe, a Native American from Oklahoma, won the pentathlon and the decathlon. To win the pentathlon, he had to make the best-combined score in five track and field events. The decathlon consisted of ten events. Thorpe was widely hailed in 1912 as the world's greatest all-around athlete. All this changed in 1913 when it was discovered that Thorpe had once received $15 a week to play minor league baseball, at that time a non-Olympic sport. He was stripped of his awards, and they were sent back to the Olympic Games officials who offered them to the second-place winners of the events. Both second place winners refused Thorpe's gold medals.

Despite the controversy, Jim Thorpe was voted by sportswriters in 1950 as the greatest American athlete of the 20th century. In 1973, 20 years after the champion's death, his amateur status was reinstated by the American Athletic Union. Jim Thorpe is the most famous example of Olympic Games Committee's enforcement of the discontinued rule allowing only amateur athletes as competitors.

Answer the following questions.

1. What lessons from each of these stories can be learned?

2. What makes an Olympic athlete great? Is it always winning? Why or why not?

3. What Olympic quality do these stories show?

4. How do you think these stories might inspire other Olympic hopefuls?

5. Which is your favorite story? Why?

Researching an Athlete

Select an Olympic athlete whom you would like to research. Once you have selected an Olympic athlete, you are ready to begin. Use this page to organize your research and information.

Name:

Date of birth:

Place of birth:

Competing/competed for this country:

Language spoken:

Sport/athletic event:

Background/experience: _____

_____

_____

Career highlights/interesting information: _____

_____

_____

_____

_____

Olympic Hall of Fame

Does the athlete you studied deserve to be in the Olympic Hall of Fame? Draw a picture of your athlete competing in his/her sport and post it on an "Olympic Hall of Fame" bulletin board.

Name of athlete: _____ Country: _____

Major accomplishments of this athlete: _____

_____

_____

_____

_____

Obstacles to Success

Think before answering the following questions. Write your answers on a separate piece of paper.

1. Define greatness. What is it? What does it look like?

2. What characteristics does an Olympic athlete need to have? What makes an Olympic athlete great?

3. What do you think motivates a great Olympic athlete?

4. Is it the same thing(s) that motivated ancient Olympic athletes?

5. Define the word *obstacle*. What is it? What does an obstacle look like?

6. List any obstacles that an Olympic athlete might have to face in the following areas:

   a. emotional   c. financial

   b. physical   d. political.

7. Can you identify any Olympic athletes who have overcome some of these obstacles?

8. What were these obstacles? How did they overcome them? Write at least one example.

9. Now look at yourself. What makes you great? What qualities and talents do you possess?

10. What goals do you have? List at least five.

11. What obstacles might prevent you from accomplishing your goals?

12. What can you do to overcome these obstacles? Tell about your plan.

13. How will you know what success looks like? Write a narrative about a personal experience you have had with a goal, an obstacle, and finally success. Remember, a narrative is written in first person about a personal experience. Check your spelling, punctuation, and handwriting. Make it great!

Letter to an Olympic Athlete

Select an Olympic athlete that you admire from the past or present. If you could send a letter to this person, what would you say? Read the sample letter below. On a separate piece of paper, write your own imaginary letter to the Olympic athlete you have chosen. Don't forget to use the parts of a letter. These parts are the date, the address, greeting, body of the letter, closing, and signature.

September 16, 2005

Clifton Cushman
1349 Hidden Canyon Road
Los Angeles, CA 98674

Dear Mr. Cushman,

I have just read an article about your experience competing for the 1964 Olympic team. I bet you were frustrated and upset when you fell during the hurdle race, but your example after the race is even more important to young people like me.

Thanks for setting a good example for us and letting us know that winning isn't everything. You are an amazing athlete! I can't believe what you were able to do.

I want you to know that I have a lot of respect and admiration for you. I wish I could tell you how impressed I am with your ability to keep giving it your best! Keep up the great work! I am one of your biggest fans.

Sincerely,

Jane Jensen

Jane Jensen

Olympic Events

In what sports and events do Olympic athletes compete? The International Olympic Committee chooses the disciplines, events, and sports for each Olympic Games.

✥ **Disciplines** are a branch of an Olympic sport comprising one or several events.

Example: An example of a discipline would be aquatics. Athletes compete in many events that fall under the heading of aquatics.

✥ **Events** are competitions in an Olympic sport or in one of the disciplines.

Example: An event is a contest in a sports program. For example, there are eight events in the diving sport under the discipline of aquatics. **Note:** *In the chart below, the number of events are listed in parentheses.*

✥ An Olympic **sport** is widely practiced by men in at least 75 countries and on four continents and by women in at least 25 countries and on three continents. Some sports have separate events while others have just one.

Example: An example of an Olympic sport would be diving. Diving is a sport under the discipline of aquatics. Another example of a sport would be a game like soccer or basketball.

Olympic Games

Aquatics (44)	Modern Pentathlon (2)
Diving (8)	Rowing (14)
Synchronized Swimming (2)	Sailing/Yachting (11)
Water Polo (2)	Shooting (17)
Archery (4)	Soccer (Football) (2)
Athletics (Track & Field) (46)	Softball (1)
Badminton (5)	Table Tennis (4)
Baseball (1)	Taekwondo (8)
Basketball (2)	Team Handball (2)
Boxing (12)	Tennis (4)
Canoe/Kayak (16)	Triathlon (2)
Cycling (18)	Volleyball (4)
Equestrian (6)	Weightlifting (15)
Fencing (10)	Wrestling (16)
Field Hockey (2)	Freestyle (8)
Gymnastics (18)	Greco-Roman (8)
Judo (14)	

Olympic Winter Games

Biathlon (6)
Bobsled (2)
Curling (2)
Figure Skating (4)
Singles (2)
Pairs (1)
Dance (1)
Hockey (2)
Luge (3)
Skiing (33)
Alpine (10)
Combined (2)
Freestyle (4)
Nordic (10)
Ski Jumping (3)
Snowboarding (4)
Speed Skating (16)
Long Track (10)
Short Track (6)

Extension: What criteria do you think the IOC uses to determine which sports or events should be added to the Olympic Games? Make a list of these criteria. What events or sports do you think should be added to the Olympic Games? Be sure to justify your answers.

Comparing the Games

The Olympic Winter Games made their debut in 1924. The first Olympic Winter Games were held in Chamonix, France. What is the difference between the Olympic Games and the Olympic Winter Games? Use the Venn diagram below to list the similarities and differences. Place the similarities in the center where the two circles connect.

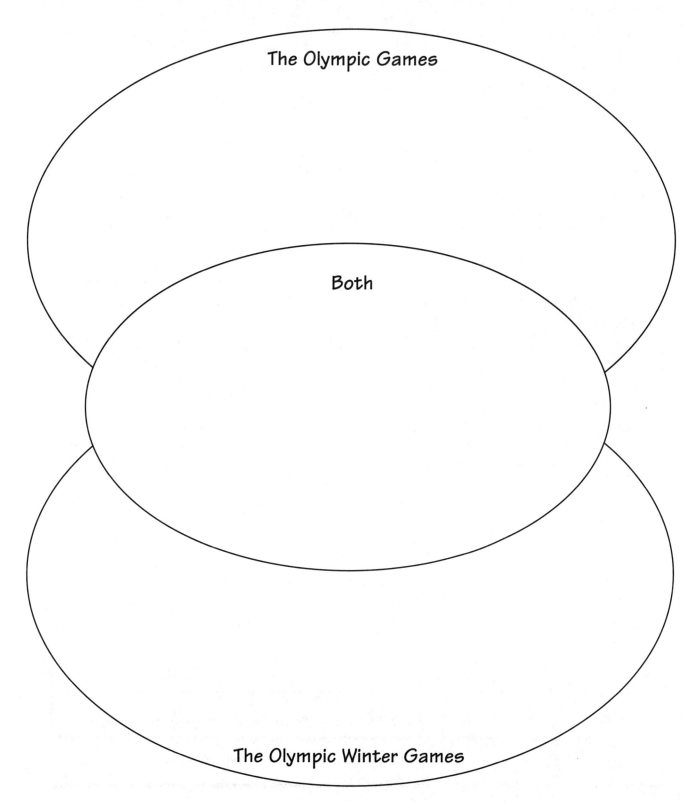

History of Olympic Sports

What is the history of the sports of the Olympic Games? We know that the first Olympic event was a running race. Through the years, more and more sports have been added to the Olympic schedule. Read the history of the following sports:

✛ Basketball

Basketball was invented in 1891 by Dr. James Naismith, a physical education teacher. The first game used a soccer ball and two peach baskets as goals attached to a 10-foot high railing. In the beginning, there were no free throws or dribbling. Basketball became an Olympic sport in 1936. Women's basketball was added as a medal sport in 1976.

✛ Athletics

Athletics is the name for Olympic events that include running, jumping, and throwing. Athletics (track and field) events began with a short race at the first modern Olympic Games. Other events, like the javelin, discus, and long jump, were added later. Track events include all foot races. Field events include jumping and throwing. The events are held on outside tracks.

✛ Baseball

The first baseball game was held in Hoboken, New Jersey, in 1846. There were two teams of nine players. The men hit a ball with a bat and ran around the bases to score points. Nowadays, millions of people around the world attend baseball games each year. There are two professional major leagues in the United States. Baseball was made a medal sport in the Olympic Games of 1992.

✛ Figure Skating

Figure skating became an Olympic sport in 1908. The skaters must perform difficult moves, jumps, and spins. An American named Jackson Haines added ballet, music, and colorful costumes to the sport of ice-skating. Pair skating began in Vienna, Austria, in the 1880s. The partners perform difficult throws and lifts. Ice dancing became an Olympic sport in 1976.

✛ Gymnastics

Fredrich Ludwig Jahn, a German, is the father of modern gymnastics. He invented the parallel bars, horizontal bar, balance beam, pommel horse, and the rings. Gymnasts compete as a team and also as individuals. Men's gymnastics became an Olympic sport in 1896. Women's gymnastics became an Olympic sport in 1928. The sport of rhythmic gymnastics for women was added to the Olympic Games in 1984.

Extension: Select another Olympic sport not mentioned above. Research to learn more about the history of this sport and when it was added as a medal sport of the Olympic Games. Record your findings on a separate piece of paper.

Create an Olympic Sport

Olympic sports and events are added to the Olympic Games all the time. Create an Olympic sport that you think would be popular at the Olympic Games. Answer the questions to describe your Olympic creation. Remember this must be a sport or event never seen at the Olympic Games before. Look at the list of Olympic sports/events on page 56 for reference.

1. What is the name of your sport/event? _____

2. What is the objective? _____

_____

3. What are the rules and directions? _____

_____

_____

4. What uniform or equipment would athletes need?_____

_____

_____

5. What judges or officials will be needed? _____

_____

_____

6. Describe the scoring system._____

_____

7. Draw a picture of athlete(s) competing in your sport/event.

Games on Ice

Did you know that all of the Winter Olympic sports require snow or ice? How is an athlete able to move quickly across the ice or in the snow? How does an athlete stop on ice or snow? Ice and snow are made of water. Use this page to demonstrate to your students how ice is made and how it can be used to create some of the most popular Olympic spectator sports.

Water is one of the few known substances that naturally exists on Earth as a gas (otherwise known as *vapor*), a solid, and a liquid.

gas = *vapor*   **solid** = *ice*   **liquid** = *water*

1. Show water in the different forms and stages. You can show water as a vapor by heating a pot of water on a hot plate. The steam rising off the top is the vapor. Pour water into an ice tray and have the students put it in a freezer. Pull it out later to check the process of freezing. Remove it the next day to show the solid ice.

2. Ice is a unique solid because it has very little friction. This lack of friction allows things to slide and is a requirement for all Winter Olympic sports. To demonstrate this, freeze a thin layer of water in a cookie sheet. Have the students take turns trying to slide a penny across the ice, across a piece of carpeting, across a piece of sandpaper, and across their desktops. They will discover that the penny glides the easiest (the farthest) on the ice.

3. Discuss friction with your students. Friction is a force trying to stop movement between two surfaces. Which of the surfaces from question #2 had the most friction? Why do you think so? Which surface had the least friction? Why do you think this is?

4. When something moves across ice, its weight pushes down on the ice and makes it temporarily melt. This reduces friction and enables skaters, bobsled runners, and luge sleds to glide over the ice quickly. The ice melts under the runners of the skates or sled. As soon as the weight passes over, the ice refreezes if the temperature is low enough.

5. Ask students to predict what will happen when ice cubes melt. Use a glass filled with ice cubes. Most will think the glass will overflow. Set the glass with ice aside and check it later in the day when the ice has completely melted. Explain that it did not overflow because the water from the ice takes up less space than the ice cube did.

6. If possible, show a video of a figure skater gliding across the ice and a skier skiing down a mountain. How does the skater stop and start? How does the skier use the skis to stop and start? What makes the skis go down the hill faster? Slower?

> **Extension:** Invite an athlete who participates in winter sports to your class. Ask the athlete to share what he or she knows about moving on ice and snow. What does it feel like? What makes it difficult?

Who Is in First Place?

In every Olympic Games, the work of the judges is most important. In some sports, their opinions determine, the medal. Racing events were judged by eye until the 1912 Olympic Games when the electrical timing device was introduced. The 1932 Los Angeles Olympic Games brought electronic scoring. Today, measuring devices are very accurate. The difference between a gold and silver medal can be measured in a few hundredths of a second.

1. Below are scores for a pair figure skating team. Write the scores from least to greatest.

| 5.6 | 5.5 | 5.7 | 5.8 | 5.9 | 5.8 |

_____   _____   _____   _____   _____   _____

2. Look at these scores for a freestyle swimming race. Rewrite the numbers from least (the winner) to the greatest. Then subtract each number from the time just above to find the difference in the finishing times. To check your answers, add each of your differences. If your sum equals the target number, you deserve a gold medal!

Time	Fastest	Diff.
51.70		
51.89		
49.99		
51.79		
50.81		
51.68		
	Target = 1.90	

3. Now, do the same times for the breaststroke, the backstroke, and the butterfly swimming races:

Butterfly

Time	Fastest	Diff.
55.09		
55.81		
54.65		
54.50		
55.11		
	Target = 1.46	

Breaststroke

Time	Fastest	Diff.
1:04.37		
1:03.43		
1:03.11		
1:04.23		
1:04.38		
1:04.26		
	Target = 1.27	

Backstroke

Time	Fastest	Diff.
55.49		
56.34		
57.69		
57.49		
57.22		
	Target = 2.20	

4. Which race had the closest finish? _____

OLYMPIC VENUE

4

THE OLYMPIC
EXPERIENCE
IN YOUR SCHOOL

The Olympic Experience

As a culminating activity for your students, you are now ready to move to the last venue. In Venue 4, you will be putting on the Olympic Games in your school. This can be done as a class or as a school. These directions are for hosting the Olympic Games as a class. See page 79–80 for instructions on how to adapt this activity for a school-wide experience. Don't forget to have students add their venue #4 stickers to their Olympic Passport when the Class Olympic Games are completed.

Your students will have fun staging their own Olympic Games. This will take dedication and hard work. All students will be involved in competing in and organizing the Olympic Games. Each student will be placed on a team and a committee. The directions and instructions needed to stage these Olympic Games will follow on the next few pages of this unit. Below is a suggested map of how to set up these Olympic Games.

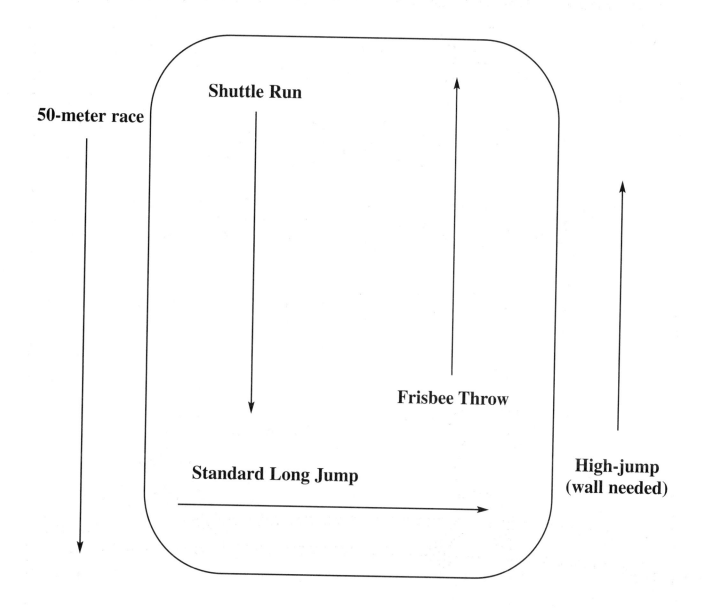

Creating a Team

Divide your class into groups of five students. It will work best if there are no more than five teams in your classroom. If you have more than 25 students, you can add to the teams, making them as equal as possible. Be sure to take academic and athletic ability into consideration when forming teams. The teams should have a nice balance. Once the teams have been created, they are ready to get organized!

Team Name

Each team needs a name. Have students work together to brainstorm names and determine the names for their teams. Each team can have a mascot, if desired.

Team Color

Each team will be assigned a color. The colors correspond with the rings on the Olympic flag. Students will want to use this color to create team identity.

➣ **Red**   *Team 1*   Team name: _____

➣ **Yellow**   *Team 2*   Team name: _____

➣ **Black**   *Team 3*   Team name: _____

➣ **Blue**   *Team 4*   Team name: _____

➣ **Green**   *Team 5*   Team name: _____

At the Opening Ceremonies, each team will be required to wear its team color. This will help identify who belongs on what team.

Team Flag

Once the team name and color have been established, teams are ready to design and create a team flag. Teams can put their mascots on their flags. Using white construction paper (or white material) and colored markers, students can make their flags. They will need one large flag to carry into the Opening Ceremonies, and they can make smaller flags for each team member to use, as well. When the flags are completed, mount them on wooden dowels so they are easy to carry. Make sure that all of the official team flags are the same size.

Team Cheer

Team members should work together to come up with a team cheer. This cheer will be used to encourage and cheer on team members while they are competing at the Olympic Games.

The Olympic Torch

As teams, have students work together to make torches. These torches can be carried at the Opening Ceremonies, as well. A torch can be made by coloring the pattern on page 89, or students can make a torch by fastening a crumpled piece of orange tissue paper to the inside of an empty paper-towel tube.

Olympic Day Schedule

There are two parts to our Olympic Games: the Athletic Olympic Games and the Academic Olympic Games. This schedule lists both of these events in one day. You may choose to hold the Athletic Olympic Games one day and the Academic Olympic Games the next. Feel free to make adjustments in the times, the events, and the schedule. This is a sample schedule only. Descriptions of the individual and team events are on pages 66–68.

8:30 A.M.	Opening Ceremonies
	Individual Events (*Students will participate in one event only*)
9:00 A.M.	Boys' 50-meter dash
	Girls' 50-meter dash
9:30 A.M.	Girls' Frisbee Throw
	Boys' Frisbee Throw
10:00 A.M.	Boy's Standing Long Jump
	Girls' Standing Long Jump
10:30 A.M.	Girls' High Jump
	Boys' High Jump
11:00 A.M.	Boys' Shuttle Run
	Girls' Shuttle Run
11:30 A.M.	Lunch Break
	Team Events (*All students will compete in teams.*)
12:00 P.M.	Boys' 4 x 50-meter relay (4 members per team—1 member cheers)
	Girls' 4 x 50-meter relay (4 members per team—1 member cheers)
12:30 P.M.	Soccer Game (*All members of each team participate.*)
1:30 P.M.	Academic Olympic Games (*See page 71 for directions.*)
2:00 P.M.	Awards Ceremony and Closing Ceremonies

Extension: You may wish to try other games and events. Other athletic-event suggestions include a volleyball game, swimming races, basketball game, kickball game, three-legged races, and other running races. You could also host an Olympic Games featuring the Olympic sports and events created by the students.

Athletic Olympic Event Descriptions

Individual Events

✤ 50-meter Dash

Materials Needed: measuring tape, cones indicating start and finish line, stopwatches, whistle, flag (optional), event record sheet, pencil

Directions: Using the measuring tape, measure 50 meters on your playground or field. For the most accurate results, each runner will have to run and be timed individually. If time does not allow this, you can have a group of runners and a volunteer to time each runner. If you do not have a stopwatch, you may start all of the runners at the same time and make a visual judgement about the first three finishers. The whistle can be the sound for the runners to "go." The flag can be waved as the runners cross the finish line.

Help Needed: This event will need a volunteer at the starting line explaining to the runners where they are running and how they will start the race. This volunteer will work closely with the other volunteers at the finish line. At the finish line, you will need a stopwatch and volunteer for each runner. The three fastest runners will receive the gold, silver, and bronze medals.

✤ Frisbee Throw

Materials Needed: masking tape to mark the starting point, five or more Frisbees, a measuring tape, event record sheet, pencil, and marker

Directions: Each athlete stands on the starting point and throws the Frisbee as far as he or she can. The athlete is not allowed to get a running start. Judges in the field use masking tape to mark the landing spot of each Frisbee. The student's initials are written on the masking tape. Each athlete will have three tries to throw the Frisbee as far as he or she can. When all of the Frisbees have been thrown, the judges will measure the longest distance for each athlete. The top three longest distances will receive the gold, silver, and bronze medals.

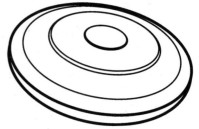

Help Needed: Ideally, this event needs at least two volunteers. These two volunteers will serve as judges and measure the distance that athletes were able to throw the Frisbees. Judges will record the top five distances on the event record sheet.

Athletic Olympic Event Descriptions *(cont.)*

Individual Events *(cont.)*

✛ Standing Long Jump

Materials Needed: masking tape to mark the jumping point, measuring tape or meter stick, event record sheet, pencil

Directions: Each athlete will have three tries to jump from a marked starting line. There will be no running prior to the jump. The athlete must stand on the designated line and jump. The athletes can use their arms to propel themselves forward. The judges will then measure the jumps with a measuring tape or stick. Keep a record of the jumps for each athlete. The three athletes with the farthest jumps will be awarded the gold, silver, or bronze medals. If an athlete falls backwards or steps over the line, the attempt is disqualified.

Help Needed: A minimum of two volunteers are needed to serve as judges. One judge will stand at the line holding one end of the measuring tape while the other judge measures the length of the jump. One of the judges will need to record the top five jumps on the record sheet.

✛ High Jump

Materials Needed: wall (preferably an outdoor wall that can be written on with chalk), chalk, measuring tape, event record sheet, pencil

Directions: Each athlete will stand next to a wall with a piece of chalk in his or her hand. The athlete then jumps up as high as possible, and marks the wall with the chalk. Each athlete will have three tries at jumping. The judge will measure the highest jump for each athlete. The three athletes with the highest jumps will be awarded the gold, silver, or bronze medals.

Help Needed: This event needs a minimum of one volunteer. This volunteer will serve as a judge to make sure athletes are jumping correctly and to also measure the height of each jump.

✛ Shuttle Run

Materials Needed: masking tape to mark start/finish line and turn-around line, block or other small item, stopwatch, event record sheet, pencil

Directions: Judges mark 15 feet from the starting line to the finish line. The athlete will start at the start line. The block is placed at the turn-around line. At the word "Go," the athlete will run to the turn-around line, pick up the block, and race back across the finish line. The athlete must cross the turn-around line before returning. If the block is dropped, the run is disqualified. The athlete has two runs. The athlete with the fastest run will win the gold.

Help Needed: This race needs two volunteers. These volunteers serve as judges. The judges will tell the athletes when to go and the judges will time the runners. Only the fastest times are recorded.

Athletic Olympic Event Descriptions *(cont.)*

Team Events

❖ 4 x 50-meter Relay

Materials Needed: masking tape to mark the start/finish points for each runner, five batons (one for each team), measuring tape to measure 50-meter segments on the track or field, whistle, stopwatches (one for each team), event record sheet

Directions: This race is run by four people. It is a relay race. Each runner is spaced 50 meters apart. Each runner will run 50 meters and then pass the baton on to the next runner. The next runner cannot go until he or she has the baton. This race should consist of both boys and girls. Each team will select four runners to race in the relay, and one (or more) team members to cheer on the sidelines for the team.

Help Needed: The relay race will need volunteers to help at the starting and finish lines and one at each passing of the baton. The volunteers at the starting line will get the first runners ready to race and will blow the whistle when it is time for the race to begin. The volunteers spaced at the different baton exchange locations will watch to ensure that the batons are passed correctly, that the runners do not leave without taking the baton, and that no batons are dropped. If the baton is dropped, the team is disqualified.

The volunteers at the finish line have the stopwatches and time each of the teams. The times are recorded. A gold medal will go to each member of the winning team. The same goes for the second-place silver team and the third-place bronze team.

❖ Soccer Game

Materials Needed: soccer balls, soccer nets, referees, whistle, tape or chalk to make boundary lines, timers

Directions: Create the boundaries for the playing field using chalk or tape. Set the soccer nets up at either end. Write the names of each team on a slip of paper. Put these slips of paper into a bowl. Draw two names out of the bowl. These two teams will be the first to play against each other. Review soccer rules with the teams. The timer will be set for fifteen minutes. The two teams have fifteen minutes to score as many goals as possible. Once the time is up, the score is recorded and the next two teams play against each other. The team that was able to score the most points (regardless of which team they played) is the gold medal team. The team with the next highest amount of points receives the silver, and the third highest receives the bronze. Not all teams will play each other.

Help Needed: You will need volunteers to referee the soccer games and keep track of the goals that are scored. You can have more than one game going on at the same time if you have enough referees and enough outdoor space.

Athletic Olympic Event Student Sign-Up

You are allowed to sign up for one individual event. Only one student per team can compete in each individual event, unless you have permission from your teacher. Sign your name below, next to the event in which you will be competing.

Boys' 50-meter dash

1. _____
2. _____
3. _____
4. _____
5. _____

Girls' 50-meter dash

1. _____
2. _____
3. _____
4. _____
5. _____

Girls' Frisbee Throw

1. _____
2. _____
3. _____
4. _____
5. _____

Boys' Frisbee Throw

1. _____
2. _____
3. _____
4. _____
5. _____

Boys' Standing Long Jump

1. _____
2. _____
3. _____
4. _____
5. _____

Girls' Standing Long Jump

1. _____
2. _____
3. _____
4. _____
5. _____

Girls' High Jump

1. _____
2. _____
3. _____
4. _____
5. _____

Boys' High Jump

1. _____
2. _____
3. _____
4. _____
5. _____

Boys' Shuttle Run

1. _____
2. _____
3. _____
4. _____
5. _____

Girls' Shuttle Run

1. _____
2. _____
3. _____
4. _____
5. _____

Olympic Event Record Sheet

Use this page to record the results of the Olympic events. Write the names of the top five finishers in each event.

Boys' 50-meter dash

Gold: _____

Silver: _____

Bronze: _____

4th Place:_____

5th Place:_____

Girls' 50-meter dash

Gold: _____

Silver: _____

Bronze: _____

4th Place:_____

5th Place:_____

Girls' Frisbee Throw

Gold: _____

Silver: _____

Bronze: _____

4th Place:_____

5th Place:_____

Boys' Frisbee Throw

Gold: _____

Silver: _____

Bronze: _____

4th Place:_____

5th Place:_____

Boys' Standing Long Jump

Gold: _____

Silver: _____

Bronze: _____

4th Place:_____

5th Place:_____

Girls' Standing Long Jump

Gold: _____

Silver: _____

Bronze: _____

4th Place:_____

5th Place:_____

Girls' High Jump

Gold: _____

Silver: _____

Bronze: _____

4th Place:_____

5th Place:_____

Boys' High Jump

Gold: _____

Silver: _____

Bronze: _____

4th Place:_____

5th Place:_____

Boys' Shuttle Run

Gold: _____

Silver: _____

Bronze: _____

4th Place:_____

5th Place:_____

Girls' Shuttle Run

Gold: _____

Silver: _____

Bronze: _____

4th Place:_____

5th Place:_____

Academic Olympic Event

Make copies of this page and have students read the rules and directions. Be sure to discuss any questions that may arise.

Object of the Academic Event

The academic Olympic event does not test physical skill, rather it tests mental skill. Each team will compete against other teams for the correct answer. Questions will be asked in order. If a team answers a question incorrectly, this question is given to the next team to answer. The team with the most points at the end of the game is declared the winner and receives the gold medal.

Setting Up the Game

Each team will select a speaker. Only the team speaker can give the answer. Team members can consult with one another to answer the question, but only the speaker for the team can say the answer. Each team will sit at a table. Team points are recorded on the board for everyone to see. Teams will have 30 seconds to discuss the question with team members. When the 30 seconds are up, the speaker for the team must give the answer right away.

The questions that are asked during this academic Olympic event are about topics and information the students have studied throughout this unit. There will also be some questions that are student-driven. The teacher or parent helper will be the judge. Students will need to understand that what the judge decides must stand and there will be no arguing. The game is over once a predetermined number of questions have been answered, or a designated amount of time (45 minutes to one hour) has taken place.

Game Preparation

Prior to the beginning of the game, students will work as a team to create three questions. These questions may or may not be asked during the course of the game, and there is no guarantee which team will end up answering these questions. The questions and answers should be recorded below.

Question #1: _____

_____

Answer: _____

Question #2: _____

_____

Answer: _____

Question #3: _____

_____

Answer: _____

Academic Olympic Event Questions

The questions on this page, as well as those on page 73, should be used in the Academic Olympic Event Contest. You should read and preview all questions prior to the start of the game. Answers are listed in italics.

1. When were women first allowed to compete in the Olympic Games? *(1900, in the sport of lawn tennis)*

2. What were the only years that the Olympic Games were not held? *(during the World Wars: 1916, 1940, and 1944)*

3. Which country's team is the first to walk in the Opening Ceremonies? *(the athletes from Greece)*

4. What animal was the first Olympic mascot? *(a dachshund, which is a breed of dog)*

5. What do the rings on the Olympic flag stand for? *(the continents that participate in the Olympic Games)*

6. What must a city have to host the Olympic Winter Games? *(snow)*

7. In which sport did Carl Lewis compete? *(track and field)*

8. In which sport did Jim Abbott compete? *(baseball)*

9. Name two cities in the United States that have hosted the Olympic Games. *(choose from Los Angeles, St. Louis, Atlanta, Squaw Valley, Lake Placid, Salt Lake City)*

10. What is used to light the Olympic flame? *(the Olympic torch)*

11. What is the prize for second place at the Olympic Games? *(silver medal)*

12. Who participated in the ancient Olympic Games? *(only men and boys)*

13. In what year did the ancient Olympic Games begin? *(approximately 776 B.C.)*

14. How many years are there between the Summer and Winter Games? *(since 1992, there are two years)*

15. In which country did the modern Olympic Games begin? *(Athens, Greece)*

16. What did winners in the ancient Olympic Games receive? *(olive wreaths)*

17. What is a chariot? *(a two-wheeled carriage pulled by four horses)*

18. Who carries the flag of each team into the stadium? *(a member of the team chosen by teamates)*

Academic Olympic Event Questions *(cont.)*

See page 72 for instructions. Answers are listed in italics.

19. Which Olympic Games has more events, summer or winter? *(summer)*

20. Who leads the athletes in reciting the Olympic Oath? *(usually one of the athletes from the host city)*

21. What country held the Olympic Winter Games in Calgary? *(Canada)*

22. What country held the first Olympic Winter Games? *(France)*

23. What country has hosted the most Olympic Games? *(United States of America)*

24. What did the ancient judges wear? *(purple robes)*

25. What did the five rings stand for in ancient Greece? *(the number of years between the Olympic Games)*

26. What is one of the words in the Olympic motto in English? *(Swifter, Higher, Stronger)*

27. Who first entered the arena during the ancient Games? *(the judges)*

28. Why are doves sometimes released at the Olympic Games? *(to symbolize peace)*

29. When is the Olympic flame lit? *(during the Opening Ceremonies)*

30. Why did mostly U.S. athletes attend the St. Louis Olympic Games? *(travel was difficult for most athletes)*

31. Name a country that has hosted both Summer and Winter Games? *(France, U.S., Japan, Canada, and Italy)*

32. What is an event that uses a pole? *(pole vault and skiing)*

33. Name one Alpine skiing event. *(downhill, slalom, giant slalom)*

34. How does a gymnast use a horse? *(men and women's vaulting, men's pommel horse routine)*

35. Name three swimming events. *(butterfly, backstroke, breaststroke, and freestyle)*

36. Who was Jesse Owens? *(U.S. track star in the 1936 Olympic Games)*

37. What is the longest race in the Olympic Games? *(the marathon)*

38. Who was Baron de Coubertin? *(founder of the Modern Olympic Games)*

39. What was a stade? *(the length of the stadium—approximately 180 meters)*

40. Who was Hera? *(a Greek goddess who was the wife of Zeus)*

Olympic Committees

Staging a class or school Olympic Games requires the help of all students. Assigning each student to a committee allows all students to work together to bring about this exciting event. Assign groups of students to work on committees different than the teams used for the Olympic Games. This allows students to work with other students and gives fair representation to all of the teams on the committees. Listed below are the responsibilities for each committee. There are five committees. Assign one student to be the manager of each committee.

✢ Decorating and Advertising Committee

Materials Needed: white construction paper, markers, wooden dowels, crepe paper, balloons (*optional*)

Directions: The responsibility for this committee is to advertise the Olympic Games around the school for classes that may want to come and watch. Posters listing the times, dates, and locations need to be made to promote the Olympic events.

Committee members will also need to make decorations to help create the Olympic spirit. Students can make Olympic flags that can be hung and placed in the area of the Olympic Games and at the Opening and Closing Ceremonies. They can also decorate the site for the Opening and Closing Ceremonies with crepe paper and balloons, if desired.

✢ Documenting and Reporting Committee

Materials Needed: video camera, battery, cut cards (optional), paper, pencils

Directions: This committee is responsible for documenting the Olympic activities. It will require some coordination and time. The members will need to coordinate each other's schedules during the Olympic events so that they can each compete in an event.

This committee has varying roles. One student will be the cameraperson. This person will, with the help of an adult, do the video recording (except when he/she is competing) of the Olympic Games. Another student will be the weather person. The weather person should use maps to show the viewing audience what to expect in the way of weather for the day of the Olympic Games. You will need two or three field reporters who are stationed around the Olympic Games. These reporters can plan interviews with the athletes, both the winners and the losers. Field reporters will also search for interesting stories about these young athletes and their families. Reporters can report on the history of the events at this Olympic Games. Don't forget that the Opening and Closing Ceremonies should also be documented.

Olympic Committees *(cont.)*

Here are the instructions for the last three committees. Be sure to review these with the individual committee members. Students need a clear understanding of their assignments.

❖ Ceremony Committee

Materials Needed: CD player, musical recordings of the World Anthem and other marching/celebration music, camera, film, U.S. flag

Directions: This committee is responsible for the organization and preparations needed for the Opening and Closing Ceremonies. Students in this committee should read through the Opening and Closing Ceremonies plans on page 76.

❖ Judging and Recording Committee

Materials Needed: stopwatches, measuring sticks, parent helpers, large construction paper, markers

Directions: Under the direction of parent volunteers, this committee will be responsible for recording results and keeping score. If a student is competing, he or she will not be recording or judging.

Once the scores and times have been determined, and the recipients of gold, silver, and bronze medals are realized, this committee should create signs listing the results. These signs should be posted in a prominent place.

Teacher Note: Be sure to meet with parent volunteers prior to the day of the Olympics. You will want to review the rules and procedures for each event and to clarify how the times and distances should be counted and recorded. Be sure to answer all questions parent volunteers may have prior to the day of the Olympic Games. You will be too busy to try and clarify the rules and guidelines once the events are taking place.

❖ Celebration and Awards Committee

Materials Needed: copies of "Olympic Medals" (page 87), copies of "Olympic Certificates" (page 91), copies of "Olive Leaf Headband" (page 86), a 3-hole punch, construction paper (yellow, gray, and brown), colored markers, scissors, ribbon, cardboard (optional)

Directions: Using the copies of the pages mentioned in the materials section, students will design the gold, silver, and bronze medals. Once the designs have been created, they can be copied on colored construction paper (yellow, gray, and light brown). These can be mounted onto cardboard, if desired.

Students on this committee should make copies of the participation certificates and write student names on these. The olive-leaf headbands are optional and can be created to make headbands for medal winners.

Opening Ceremonies

✣ **Parade of Athletes**

Students will parade around the school or around the playground. They will walk with their teams, and each team will be wearing the team color previously assigned. Select one student to lead the parade. This student will carry the U.S. flag. The first person at the head of each team will carry the official team flag. The other team members can carry Olympic torches or smaller team flags. The teams will parade into the classroom or designated spot for the Opening Ceremonies. Have students set their flags on display.

✣ **Background Music**

As students participate in the Olympic parade, you can play the Olympic theme song: *World Anthems* performed by Donald Fraser and the English Chamber Orchestra. Audio CD (one disc). BMG/RCA Victor, 6321, 1998. AISN: B000007QCU. You can also play other patriotic songs or marching songs to help the mood.

✣ **Photo Opportunity**

With team members dressed in the five Olympic colors, you can arrange students in the shape of the Olympic rings and take a picture. Stand on a chair so you can get a top view of the "Olympic Rings."

✣ **Olympic Oath**

When students reach the site of the Games, lead them in reciting the Olympic Oath, pausing at each comma so that they can repeat after you:

In the name of all competitors, I promise that we shall take part in these Olympic Games, respecting and abiding by the rules that govern them, in the true spirit of sportsmanship, for the glory of the sport, and the honor of our teams.

Closing/Awards Ceremonies

✣ **Parade of Athletes**

Athletes march back to the ceremony location. Students do not walk in as teams, but they walk in with other teams and classmates. Again, you can play background music, perhaps something with an upbeat rhythm to celebrate.

✣ **Awarding of Medals**

You can present the awards and medals to the students or you can invite a guest, such as the principal, a P.E. teacher, or a special guest. The Awards Committee makes medals ahead of time. (See page 87 for medal templates.) You can also present participatory certificates (see page 91) to students who participated but did not win a medal; or you can choose to give all students a participatory certificate.

✣ **Team Cheer**

Have each team call out their team cheer and have the class clap for the effort of each team. Refreshments can be served after the parade of athletes and the awards.

Olympic News

Create a newspaper page documenting the events of the Olympic Games. Imagine that you have been assigned to be a reporter of events taking place at your Olympic Games. Use the newspaper format below for the paper.

OLYMPIC GAMES DAILY

Olympic News and Notes . . .

Meet the Athletes

Wow! Did You See That?

Olympic Happenings

Fine Arts Festival

The early members of the Olympic Games Committee did not want the Olympic Games to be merely a sports competition. From 1912 through 1948, medals were also awarded for excellence in the fine arts. The rules stated that projects were to be entered in the fields of architecture, sculpture, painting, music, and literature. The works were to be inspired by sports.

Think about a project that you could do in one of the fields above. For literature, you may wish to write a story about an athlete who works hard to make it to the Olympic Games. You may also submit a painting that portrays an athlete competing in an Olympic event or sport. Use clay, or another medium, to sculpt an athlete in action. You could also create a song that would inspire an Olympic athlete to try his or her best. Be creative! Use this form to plan your project and to get approval from your teacher.

Fine Arts Project

Name:_____

Fine Arts Field:_____

_____

_____

Project Ideas:_____

_____

Title of Selected Project: _____

_____

Description of Project: _____

_____

_____

Teacher Approval: _____

School Plan vs. Classroom Plan

You can alter the plans for the class Olympic Games to accommodate a school-wide or grade level Olympic Games. Here are some suggestions or alterations you can use to make the adjustment.

✤ Olympic Teams

With a larger group of athletes involved, you can assign each class a country to represent at the school-wide Olympic Games. Assign each country/team the responsibility to create a country flag to carry and post at the Opening Ceremonies. You can have each grade level wear an assigned color of the Olympic Rings so that you can still take a picture of the Olympic Rings formation. (You will probably have to be standing on something taller than a chair to take this picture.)

✤ Opening Ceremonies

The opening ceremonies can be easily adapted to include a larger group. Designate a parade route for all the classes willing to participate. Classes/countries will march together following their country flag. All of the athletes can take the Olympic Oath, with the principal leading the pledge.

With a larger group participating, the opening ceremonies can take on a more spectacular feel. Encourage students who are interested to create dances, songs, poetry, and other performances. These can be shared as part of the Opening Ceremonies. You can invite the school band, chorus/choir, and any other cultural clubs to perform at the ceremonies, as well.

✤ Olympic Athletic Events

With more athletes competing, you will need more time to run the athletic events. You can assign a different day for each grade level to compete. For example, kindergarten students compete on Monday, first grade on Tuesday, second grade on Wednesday, and so forth until all grade levels have had a chance to compete. You will need to award medals for each grade level, as the skills and abilities will be different, based on their ages.

✤ Olympic Academic Event

A team from each class will represent its class/country at the Academic Olympic event. You should follow the same directions as outlined on page 71.

✤ Fine Arts Festival

Select a large room such as the cafeteria or gym to display all of the student art projects. These should be completed prior to the Olympics and set up before the competition begins. This would be a nice place to hold the Opening and Closing Ceremonies.

School Plan vs. Classroom Plan *(cont.)*

✦ Parent Volunteers and Helpers

In order for a school-wide or grade-level Olympic Games to take place, you will need many parents. Teachers can meet and determine the responsibilities each class and grade level will have at the Olympic Games. These teachers can meet individually with their group of parents to explain the role and help needed from parents.

Materials: stopwatches, timers, bases, balls, and all types of materials will be needed for these Olympics. Coordinate materials with other teachers and see if the P.E. teacher can give a hand.

✦ Olympic Committees

Again, there is a lot of work for students to stage these Olympic Games. The responsibilities for each committee remain the same. See pages 74–75 for these instructions. You may choose to assign classes to be in charge of specific committees. In order to host a school-wide Olympics, you may wish to add the following committees:

1. **Information Committee**—This committee would be responsible for providing information the day of the Olympic Games. This committee can create maps of the Olympic events and direct students to where they need to be.

2. **Newspaper Committee**—This committee could actually take pictures and write newspaper articles about the sights and sounds of the Olympic Games. This newspaper could be published and distributed school-wide a few days after the Olympic Games. This keepsake could be autographed by gold medal winners.

3. **Refreshment Committee**—This committee could be responsible for providing cold water and cups to all athletes competing. If it is a hot day, this committee will be especially important so students do not need to stand in line at the drinking fountain. Be sure to have a trash receptacle handy to dispose of the paper cups.

✦ Closing Ceremonies

At the Closing Ceremonies, student athletes should walk in together. Medals and certificates should be awarded by the principal, a teacher, or another special guest. Parents can be invited to attend the ceremony. The school song could be played in conclusion, and the school mascot should be invited to attend and help celebrate!

Olympic Pictograms

Winter Sports

Biathlon

Curling

Ice Hockey

Bobsled

Figure Skating

Luge

Skiing

Snowboarding

Speed Skating

Olympic Pictograms *(cont.)*

Summer Sports

Archery

Athletics

Badminton

Baseball

Basketball

Boxing

Canoeing/Kayaking

Cycling

Olympic Pictograms *(cont.)*

Summer Sports *(cont.)*

Diving

Fencing

Gymnastics

Equestrian

Field Hockey

Judo

Modern Pentathlon

Rowing

Olympic Pictograms *(cont.)*

Summer Sports *(cont.)*

Sailing

Shooting

Soccer

Softball

Swimming

Synchronized Swimming

Table Tennis

Taekwondo

Olympic Pictograms *(cont.)*

Summer Sports *(cont.)*

Team Handball

Tennis

Triathlon

Volleyball

Weightlifting

Water Polo

Wrestling

Olive-Leaf Headbands

Color each of the leaves green. Cut out the leaves and staple them to a green construction paper headband to create an olive leaf headband.

Olympic Medals

Create designs for each of the medals below. Color one medal gold, one silver, and one bronze. Punch out the holes on each side of the tabs. Attach yarn or ribbon to create necklaces.

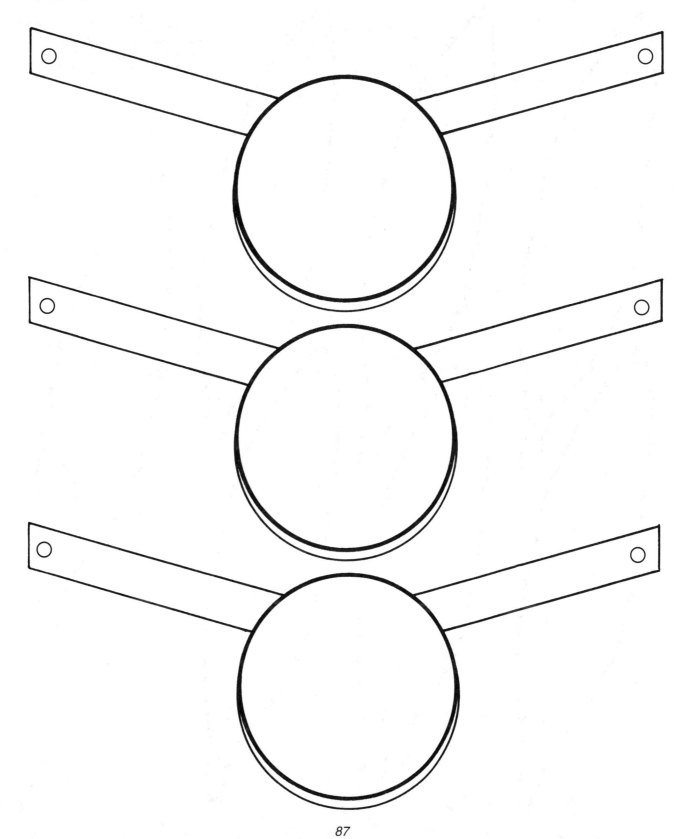

Olympic Ring

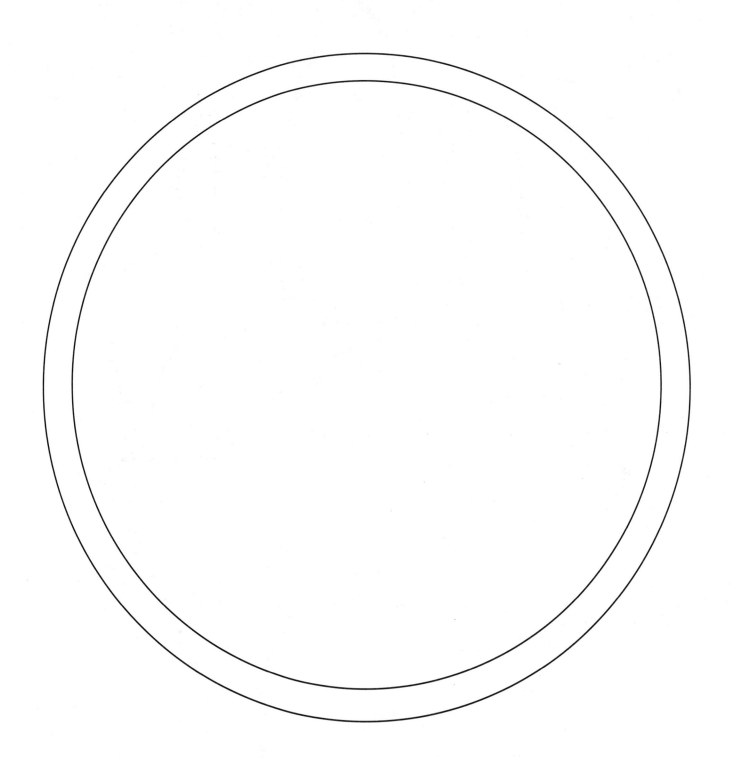

Olympic Torch

Olympic Flag

Olympic Certificate

Proud Participant in the

Mini-Olympic Games

Student's Name

Teacher/Coach

Date

World Map

Use the tab to connect pages 92 and 93.

World Map *(cont.)*

Answer Key

Page 13—Olympic Trivia

Ancient Olympic Games

1. 1900 in lawn tennis
2. only men and boys
3. 776 B.C.
4. olive wreaths
5. two-wheeled carriage pulled by four horses
6. purple robes
7. the years between the Olympic Games
8. the judges

Modern Olympic Games

9. during the World Wars: 1916, 1940, 1944
10. Greece
11. a dog
12. the continents that participate in the Olympic Games
13. snow
14. track and field
15. baseball
16. Los Angeles, St. Louis, Atlanta, Squaw Valley, Lake Placid, Salt Lake City
17. the Olympic torch
18. silver medal
19. two years
20. Greece
21. member of the team, chosen by teammates
22. summer
23. usually one of the athletes from the host city
24. France
25. USA
26. swifter, higher, stronger
27. as a symbol of peace
28. at the Opening Ceremonies
29. travel was difficult for most athletes
30. France, U.S., Japan, Canada, Italy

Page 16—The Ancient Olympic Games

Answers will vary.

Page 18—Map of Ancient Greece

1. Mt. Olympus
2. Delphi
3. Marathon
4. Athens
5. Sparta
6. Olympia
7. Corinth

Page 21—The Modern Games

1. First modern Olympic Games held in Athens, Greece
2. 1900
3. Women began to compete in lawn tennis
4. 1912
5. Women's swimming events added
6. 1924
7. 1924
8. male athletes housed in Olympic Village
9. Olympic Games first broadcast on radio
10. 1960
11. prizes awarded for fine arts and sports
12. 1992

Answer Key *(cont.)*

Page 25—The Spirit of Olympism

Accept reasonable answers.

Page 31–33—The Countries of the Olympic Games

1. Austria
2. Canada
3. France
4. Germany
5. Italy
6. Japan
7. USA
8. Switzerland
9. Australia
10. Belgium
11. Sweden
12. Finland
13. Greece
14. Mexico
15. Spain
16. South Korea
17. Russia
18. Great Britain
19. Norway
14. Netherlands

Page 41—Graphing the Medals

1. No. It lists only some of the countries that participated in the 2000 Olympic Games.

2. To compare the medal count between some of the countries that participated in 2000 Olympic Games. United States.

3. Russia

4. Italy

5. Australia, Germany, and China

Page 42—What Is the Metric System?

Answers will vary.

Page 44—Time Zones

Answers will vary.

Page 45—Money Around the World

Answers will vary.

Page 51—A Tale of an Athlete

Answers will vary.

Page 54—Obstacles to Success

Answers will vary.

Page 61—Who Is in First Place?

1. 5.5, 5.6, 5.7, 5.8, 5.8, 5.9

2.

Time	Fastest	Diff.
51.70	49.99	
51.89	50.81	.82
49.99	51.68	.87
51.79	51.70	.02
50.81	51.79	.09
51.68	51.89	.10
	Target = 1.90	1.90

3.

	Butterfly				Breaststroke				Backstroke	
Time	Fastest	Diff.		Time	Fastest	Diff.		Time	Fastest	Diff.
55.09	54.35			1:04.37	1:03.11			57.28	55.49	
55.81	54.50	.15		1:03.43	1:03.43	.32		55.49	56.34	.85
54.35	54.60	.10		1:03.11	1:04.23	.80		56.34	57.22	.88
54.65	55.09	.49		1:04.23	1:04.26	.03		57.69	57.28	.06
54.50	55.11	.02		1:04.38	1:04.37	.11		57.49	57.49	.21
55.11	55.81	.70		1:04.26	1:04.38	.01		57.22	57.69	.20
	Target = 1.46	1.46			Target = 1.27	1.27			Target = 2.20	2.20

4. .01 in the breaststroke

Bibliography

Anderson, Dave. *The Story of the Olympics.* HarperCollins Juvenile Books, 2000.

Arnold, Caroline. *Olympic Winter Games.* Franklin Watts, 1991.

———. *The Summer Olympic Games.* Franklin Watts, 1991.

Baker, William J. *Jesse Owens: An American Life.* The Free Press, 1988.

Benson, Michael. *Dream Teams.* Little, Brown, 1991.

Birenbaum, Barbara. *The Olympic Glow.* Peachtree, 1994.

Carlson, Lewis H., and John J. Fogarty. *Tales of Gold.* Contemporary Books, 1987.

Chester, David. *The Olympic Games Handbook: An Authentic History of Both the Ancient and Modern Olympics Games, Complete Results and Records.* Scribner, 1975.

Coote, James. *A Picture History of the Olympics.* Macmillan, 1972.

Crowther, Robert. *Robert Crowther's Pop-Up Olympics: Amazing Facts and Record Breakers.* Candlewick Press, 1996.

Davida, Kristy. *Coubertin's Olympics: How the Games Began.* Leiner Publications, Co., 1995.

Dershem, Kurt. *Olympians.* Iron Crown, 1990.

Duden, Jane. *Olympic.* Macmillan Child Group, 1991.

Finlay, Moses I., and H.W. Pleket. *The Olympic Games: The First Thousand Years.* Viking Press, 1976.

Hennessey, B.G. *Olympics!* Viking Penguin Books, 1996.

Holzschuler, Cynthia. *United States Olympic Committee's Curriculum Guide to the Olympic Games: The Olympic Dream.* Griffin Publishing Group/Teacher Created Materials, Inc., 2000.

Knotts, Bob. *The Summer Olympics.* Children's Press, 2000.

Ledeboer, Suzanne. *Olympism: A Basic Guide to the History, Ideals, and Sports of the Olympic Movement.* Griffin Publishing Group, 2001.

Osbourne, Mary Pope. *Hour of the Olympics.* Random House, 1998.

Oxlade, Chris, and David Ballheimer. *Eyewitness: Olympics.* Dorling Kindersley Publishing, Inc., 2000.

Web Sites

- *www.edgate.com/school_athletics/educator*
  This site offers links to various Olympic and sports-related sites.

- *www.olympics.org*
  Offers daily news updates on the Olympic Games, medal totals, and individual athletes.

- *www.usoc.org*
  This is the official web site of the United States Olympic Committee (USOC).

- *www.timeforkids.com*
  This site offers the latest information on recent or upcoming Olympic events.

- *www.sikids.com*
  This Sports Illustrated site is ranked one of the top kids' sites in Yahoo Internet Life's 100 Best Sites of 2000.